WHO'S WHO

IN CONTEMPORARY FASHION 2008

SPORTSWEAR
INTERNATIONAL

FOREWORD

AMAZINGLY OBVIOUS

"Amazing," said one of my friends in the American sportswear community when I presented him the concept and the first mock-up of this new version of Who's Who. "Amazing," he repeated, "how obvious this idea is; I really wonder why nobody has published a contemporary fashion yearbook like this before."

But that's always the case with useful ideas: they seem to be complete no-brainers when they are first presented. And, without being too modest about the results of all our brainstorming for this new product, when the finished book lies in front of you, you feel like you've done this forever. The tangible end-product is even more obvious than the idea behind it.

It's also very exciting to produce a book such as this, which focuses on the people behind a brand, an idea or an achievement: the producers, the makers, the men and women, their faces and their stories. And this year, that excitement was infectious. Take the fashion families, which are introduced under the headline "A Family Affair" in the back of the book. When we showed the first photos to our initial subjects many were so pleased and intrigued with the idea that they spontaneously told other colleagues and business friends to pose and join this exclusive club of "very important" sportswear players. We had planned to show a very limited selection of "families", 15 spreads in total, but the project kept growing, and in the end we have 26. Please take more than just a brief look at this shoot: remember, it is probably the most comprehensive photo gallery of the movers and shakers in the current sportswear market. It offers a visual and very intimate look at the sportswear families of blood or profession who give life to contemporary, young and casual fashion. And every photo in this spread tells a personal story because Italian photographer Marco La Conte grabbed his Hasselblad and traveled around the world for three months to shoot these families in their "natural environments." (And note that a special "A Family Affair" photo exhibition will be held at July's Bread&butter in Barcelona).

Another asset of this completely redesigned fashion compendium is its opening section. "The Newsmakers" are the people who lead their specific pack and brought their fashion company or group to new glorious heights within the year, the places that are inspiring to the fashion industry and the unique things or ideas that are affecting fashion today such as the organic movement, which will guide fashion to a more self-reflective and socially responsible era. Included here are also retail's best and newest, including plenty of store pictures, which let you deeply feel the mood and the atmosphere at these stunning points of sale.

Finally, this book also includes what Who's Who has always contained in its 15-year existence: a very comprehensive yet selective directory of the global sportswear market. But in this electronic age, we felt it was no longer appropriate or user-friendly to dedicate an entire printed issue to this information. So, this time, we included it on the CD that is attached on the inside back cover instead. As always, these highly useful listings were compiled meticulously by our team and include the most important brands, stores, showrooms, media, PR companies and agencies. Just slide this CD into your computer and this comprehensive and useful directory will be just a click away.

Enjoy the new Who's Who!

Klaus N. Hang
Editor & Publisher

FALKE · P.O.BOX 11 09 · D-57376 SCHMALLENBERG

FALKE

ERGONOMIC SPORT SYSTEM

THIS
IS NOT
A
DRESS
REHEARSAL

NEW YORK, NY • LOS ANGELES, CA • MANHATTAN BEAC

TRUE RELIGION
BRAND JEANS

A · CHICAGO, IL · MIAMI, FL · SHORT HILLS, NJ

BLUE

Human after all

Firetrap™
deadly denim & twisted thoughts

and fabulousity. Peace. Love. Respect.

The first family of hip hop celebrates 15 years of innovation in style.

MACY'S DEMO CARSON PIRIE SCOTT & CO. MAN ALIVE AGAINST ALL ODDS

PHAT FASHIONS™

MADE OF JAPAN

onitsukatiger.com

www.seedsofpeace.org　　www.girbaud.com

SEEDS of PEACE
EMPOWERING LEADERS OF THE NEXT GENERATION · ESTABLISHED 1993 ·

MARITHÉ
+
FRANÇOIS
GIRBAUD®

PEACE IS A FIGHT.
MARITHÉ + FRANÇOIS GIRBAUD
SUPPORTS SEEDS OF PEACE.

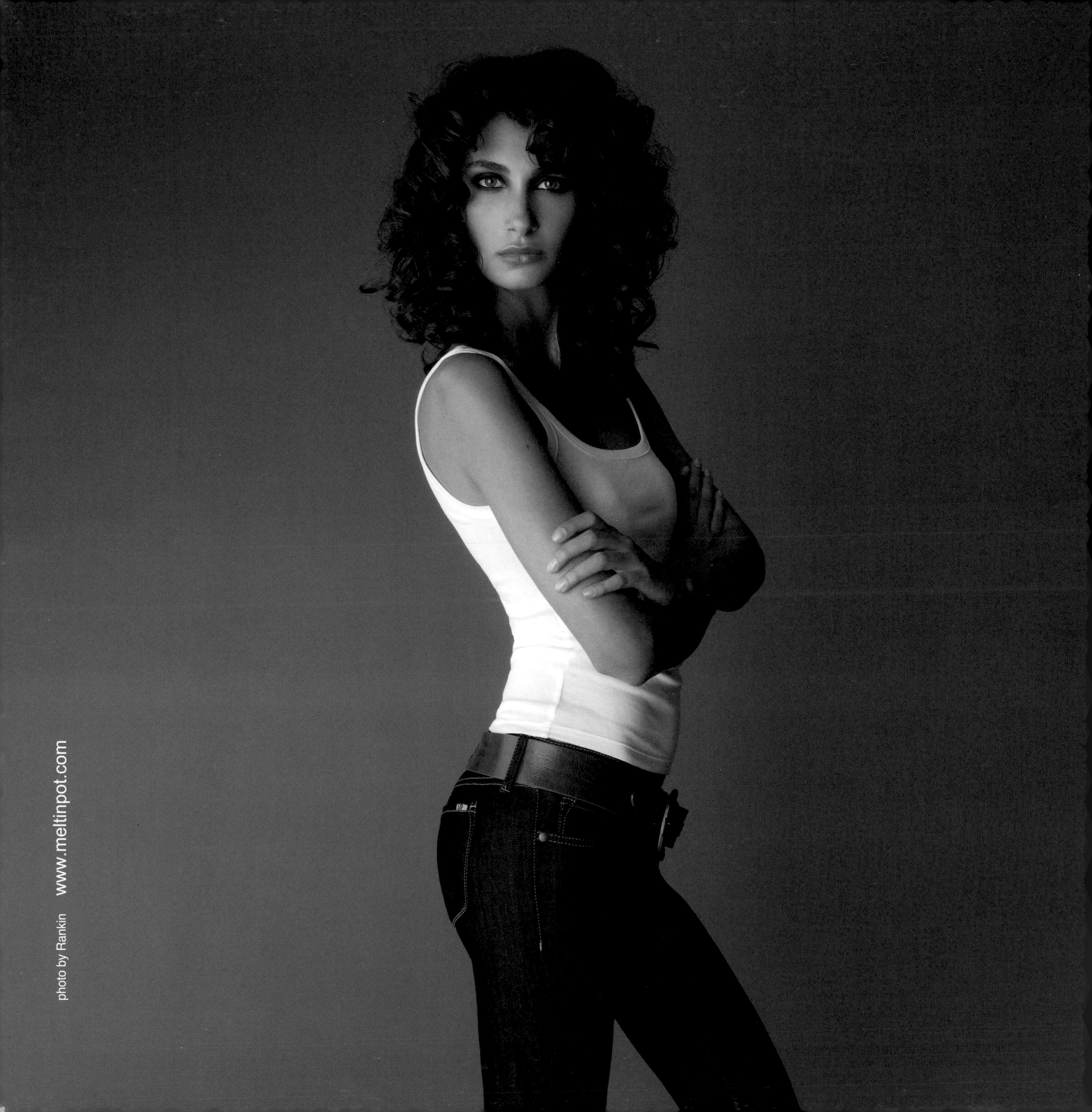
photo by Rankin
www.meltinpot.com

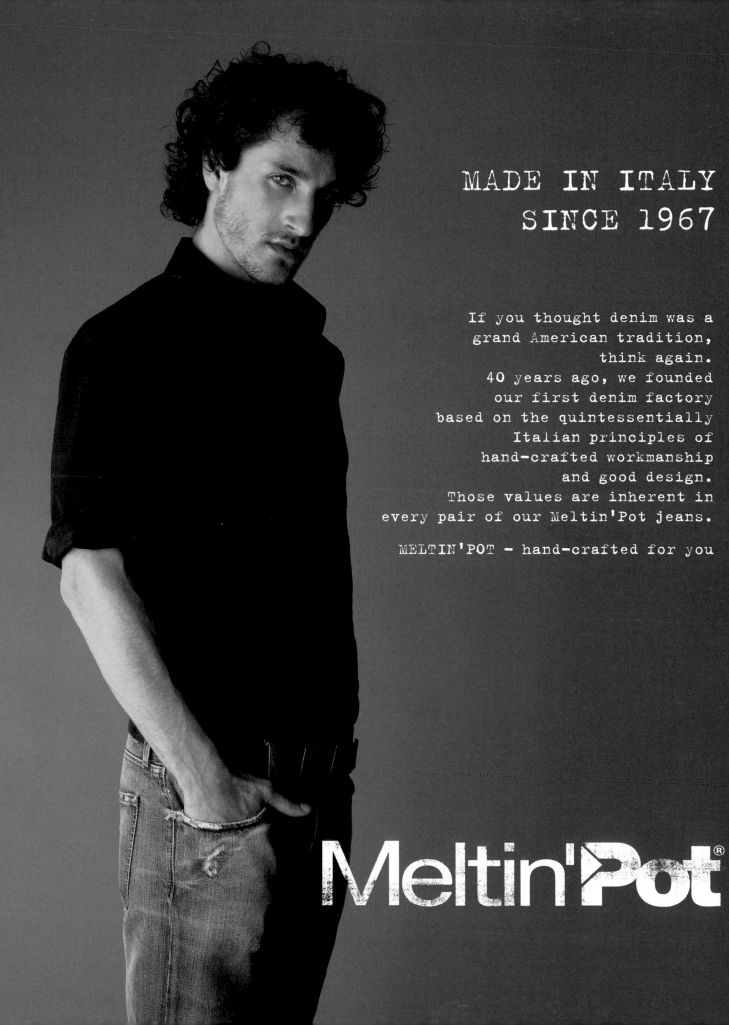

MADE IN ITALY
SINCE 1967

If you thought denim was a
grand American tradition,
think again.
40 years ago, we founded
our first denim factory
based on the quintessentially
Italian principles of
hand-crafted workmanship
and good design.
Those values are inherent in
every pair of our Meltin'Pot jeans.

MELTIN'POT - hand-crafted for you

Meltin'Pot®

TOM TAILOR *Denim*

ENK

International **Trade**

SHOWS

New York | Los Angeles | Las Vegas

ENK IntVernational | t:212.759.8055 | enkshows.com

ENK

Coterie
www.enkshows.com/coterie

solecommerce
www.enkshows.com/coterie

Collective
www.enkshows.com/collective

intermezzo
www.enkshows.com/acic

BLUE★
www.enkshows.com/blue

children's club
www.enkshows.com/childrensclub

circuit
www.enkshows.com/circut

BRIGHTE LOS ANGELES
www.enkshows.com/brighte

clear.
www.enkshows.com/clear

Brighte Vegas
www.enkshows.com/brightelv

INTRODUCTION

FASHION MAKES THE WORLD GO ROUND!

On the following pages you'll find *Sportswear International's* selection of fashion, facts and faces that are causing a stir in the business. Take a look at the controversial topics in the industry, the top fashion managers and the biggest players, the hottest trends, the most talked about brands, the freshest faces and talents, and the most inspiring stores and concepts. Let the Who's Who give you the full overview on what happens in the international fashion world ...

ECO/SOCIAL

GIVING WITH THE CLOTHES ON OUR BACKS

Words: Martine Bury

Now more than ever, fashion is political. Retailers, designers, celebrities and activists seem to have forged a new ideal for living in a material world. It's called conscious consumerism and it's apparent in a rapidly growing list of upstart eco-friendly brands, huge ones such as Gap launching its multimillion dollar (RED) campaign to help end the global AIDS crisis and retailers and other companies announcing that they are "going green."

A recent study by Colorado-based organization Lifestyles of Health and Sustainability says that, in the US alone, the market for items that help the environment and boost social justice is a booming one, estimated at $229 billion.

In fall 2006, Levi Strauss & Co. released Levi's Eco 100% organic cotton jeans in several of the familiar styles such as the Red Tab Vintage Straight Jean to trendy skinny models. The denim giant didn't stop with fabric but also utilized recycled hardware and natural indigo dye to minimize negative environmental impact. "Given our history as a leader in responsible manufacturing and business practices, this initiative

is about quality and responsibility never going out of style," said brand president Robert Hanson when it launched. American Apparel was also at the forefront of the sustainability movement with the Sustainable Edition of its cotton casualwear. Its foray into environmental activism seemed a natural progression, since it already boasts ethical anti-sweatshop fair labor practices. Likewise, Replay added organic denim for spring 2007.

Chain retailers are also getting in on the act. H&M recently launched the Organic Cotton line of tees and underwear and UK store Marks & Spencer said in January that it will spend 200 million GBP over the next five years to make all 460 of its stores carbon neutral. It also recently relabelled its clothing's care tags to promote energy-saving lower washing temperatures.

Even high-end designers are making contributions. Stella McCartney created vegan shoes and handbags and Roland Mouret made a creation for the (RED) campaign, which also boasts Emporio Armani and Converse as participants.

In the UK this year, Nike helped

launch an anti-racism wristband endorsed by soccer stars Thierry Henry and Rio Ferdinand. It is the first product of the campaign, Stand Up, Speak Up, led by Henry. "Racism is one of the biggest problems facing football across Europe," he says. "The players on the pitch need the help of all fans to help drown out the racists and tell them their actions aren't acceptable."

Green is more than just the new black. It has also proven to be fertile ground for new brands. The special edition ONE (Make Poverty History) T-shirt by Edun is manufactured in Lesotho, South Africa from 100% Africa cotton and provides much needed funds to AIDS organizations while supporting fair trade. A for-profit business that encourages the fashion community to build resources in Africa to tackle poverty, Edun has been successful due in a large part to its famous collaborators—U2's Bono, his wife Ali Hewson and designer Rogan Gregory.

Perhaps, at the end of the day, it's the grass roots movement in eco apparel that has awakened shoppers' sensibilities and opened their wallets. Independent entrepeneurs

such as Del Forte Denim, Stewart + Brown, Ekoganic and Keep Company shoes are thriving while doing their part for the betterment of the planet. "As the rest of the industry has been catching up to our eco-fashion and concept based company, our sales have tripled each season and the response to the material and quality of our collection has been incredible," says Amy Christensen, creative director of the 8-year-old Oregon-based apparel line Sameunderneath.

Even tongue-in-cheek attention has helped. Some have criticized Diesel's "Global Warming Ready" ad campaign for making light of the issue, but on its website the brand urges its customers to support stopglobalwarming.org, an online environmental watchdog.

Some critics forecasted controversy and little future impact. But that hasn't happened. "We want to change history by writing its future," said CEO Bobby Shriver at the (RED) campaign's launch. He added that by purchasing (RED) products, consumers would help a good cause. "And that's good business," Shriver said.

CHRIS ROCK IN GAP'S (RED) CAMPAIGN

041

BIJENKORF (NL)

UPTRADE/DOWNTRADE

TO AIM HIGH OR LOW?

Words: Regina Henkel

Fashion is movement and there has been a lot of movement in it of late. If recent years have been about increasing profits from core target groups, new levels of consumers are now being wooed with uptrade and downtrade concepts.

The list of retailers and labels that have made their way "upstream" is a long one. A veritable epidemic of "trading up" has broken out, especially among department stores—there is scarcely one that is not planning to add more premium fashion in the future, if it has not already done it. "We are evolving from the mainstream to the premium sector," says Marieke Heringa of the Dutch department store Bijenkorf, which now wants to offer more premium brands. Le Printemps in France is also planning to valorize its stores with more premium labels, while in March Germany's Engelhorn unveiled its new luxury accessories outlet "acc/es," featuring brands such as Celine, Loewe, Marc Jacobs and Valentino. Likewise, German department store Peek & Cloppenburg is multiplying its "Weltstadthaus" concept with grand architecture and an opulent atmosphere, and Munich's historic Ludwig Beck department store will transform entirely into an emporium dedicated purely to luxury. The changing consumer climate seems

to indicate that this is a good idea. Heringa explains, "We have felt the competition in the sector grow fiercer and we want to modify our product palette to more closely respond to the new wants and needs of our customers."

An opposite strategy is also proving popular. Beleaguered British department store Marks & Spencer, for instance, is taking advantage of a general overhaul to focus more firmly on lower price ranges—a policy that's resulting in M&S's first signs of financial amelioration in years. New York-based retailer deluxe Barneys is taking the same path, partnering up with high-street chain Topshop to feature its new Kate Moss collection and continuing to grow its hit CO-OP concept, which appeals to a younger, hipper crowd and thus has opened up a whole new price class.

All these exertions have a common aim: to seek out and capture new target groups.

In recent years the increasing verticalization of the fashion market had been causing considerable woes for retailers in the mid to lower price segments. Now, however, it seems that the verticals are not satisfied with their victory and are getting ready to conquer new target groups and new price segments. For example, H&M has raised the

stakes in the design department with spectacular cooperations with Victor & Rolf, Stella McCartney and Karl Lagerfeld. The chain's Spanish rival Inditex is pursuing a different road to success—it has long and successfully addressed a range of target groups with its portfolio of concepts, Zara, Massimo Dutti, Bershka, Pull & Bear and Oysho, and gotten wide-ranging market exploitation. Similarly, Abercrombie & Fitch added its Ruehl stores in 2004 to attract an older demographic, as did Gap with its now failed Forth & Towne concept and American Eagle Outfitters with Martin + Osa. H&M is now jumping on this bandwagon, this year opening its first COS store in London, with further branches to follow in Germany, Belgium and the Netherlands. COS is positioned in a higher quality segment than H&M. As the label's menswear designer Michael Kristensen explains: "We will be offering prêt à porter fashion at affordable prices." Men's suits will be priced between 250 and 350 Euros, leather handbags between 125 and 250 Euros.

Regarding manufacturers, Diesel has shown the denim industry how a label can go from being a fashionable denim specialist to a lifestyle brand that now charges 200 Euros per pair of jeans. In the wake of the denim boom, many new

brands have sprung up and most are not even making the attempt to hold a position in the fiercely competitive middle price segment. Jeans have thus become a luxury article—the time when denim was associated with the working class seems distant indeed. The new self-image of jeans retailers is also reflected in their increasing presence at international fashion shows. Although looks are again becoming generally more simple, and average prices have dipped to a more sensible level, brands such as G-Star, Miss Sixty and Evisu are maintaining high standards of design and now showing at New York Fashion Week. "Trading-up" is also the strategy pursued by Italian Pronto Moda label Patrizia Pepe, which just announced its intention to bring out a prêt à porter range. In sportswear and streetwear, this same policy is being implemented via partnerships with designers and artists—such as the one between Burton and the Andy Warhol Foundation.

But, as it does, fashion already has created a countertrend: Trendy yet inexpensive brands such as France's Lord Richards and Sweden's Cheap Monday and Monki (the latter is is a label and a store) have rapidly gained strong positions in their markets. Which begs the question: Might down be the new up?

Ben Sherman ®

London   New York   LA   Las Vegas   Sydney

ZERO SIZE

BODY HEAT

Words: Christopher Blomquist

The fashion industry loves to namedrop initials such as YSL, DVF and LVMH but today a far more scientific set of letters, BMI, has many tongues wagging. Short for "body mass index," a ratio of body fat based on height and weight, BMI has become a measuring stick at some fashion weeks to determine if models are too thin.

The global discussion of "zero size" began when the regional government of Madrid, which organizes and sponsors Madrid Fashion Week, or Pasarela Cibeles, announced that it would ban models with a BMI of less than 18 from the September 2006 event. Worried about endorsing overly thin figures that could potentially prompt wannabes to develop eating disorders, and reacting to the death of 20-year-old model Luisel Ramos who died of heart failure after starving herself for a fashion show in Uruguay in August, Madrid's organizers said they made their decision to promote healthy body types. As a result, 30% of the women who had walked in previous editions of the Spanish event were turned away.

While prompting some discussion and introspection in the industry, Madrid's decision hardly had a domino effect. New York Fashion Week organizers and London's British Fashion Council left it up to the designers to cast whoever they wanted for their shows and some Parisian designers dismissed the controversy as a "non-issue." As Chanel and Fendi designer Karl

Lagerfeld, who lost 90 pounds in 13 months soon after the new millennium, said on a German TV talk show: "Everybody talks about this size zero thing and anorexic models these days. I think people getting fatter is the much bigger issue and causes more trouble to the health-care system." (Perhaps

A SIZE 20 MODEL IN GAULTIER'S S/S 2007 SHOW

dismissing Lagerfeld's argument, designer Jean Paul Gaultier, literally and figuratively weighed in on the controversy by including a size 20 lingerie-clad model in his spring 2007 collection's show in Paris in October.)

Madrid's action did bring some changes, though. Milan Fashion Week's organizers also implemented a minimum BMI check and Israeli retailers announced in September 2006 that they would not hire super-skinny models for ad campaigns. Likewise, the health minister of India declared that he did not want to allow rail-like models during his country's fashion week.

The issue became even more explosive when two more South American models, 21-year-old Brazilian Ana Carolina Reston and the 18-year-old sister of Luisel Ramos, Elia-

na, died from suspected starvation-related complications in November 2006 and February 2007, respectively. Select, a modeling agency in London, announced during February 2007's London Fashion Week that it had initiated a new company policy of compulsory health checks for all 400 of its female and male models and that they would all have a doctor's certificate to prove that they were hale enough to work.

But it wasn't just at fashion weeks where people began to believe too thin was not in. A tabloid-led backlash against stick-thin celebs such as Nicole Richie, Lindsay Lohan, Mischa Barton, Kate Bosworth, Keira Knightley and Victoria Beckham emerged and rumors of anorexia, bulimia or drug-use to lose weight hounded several of these women. Rachel Zoe, the trendsetting Hollywood stylist who is widely credited for creating the popular LA tiny-body-in-giant-sunglasses-and-'70s-headscarf look, was forced to defend her own superskinny self in the press and deny accusations that she forced her famous clients such as Richie and Barton–jokingly referred to by some as the "Zoe-bots"–to lose weight. While issuing denials that she had an eating disorder, Richie fired Zoe in November 2006.

While "zero size" remains a hot-button issue in both the fashion and entertainment industries, it did take a temporary backseat to another model- and entertainment-related controversy in March 2007. The TV show *America's Next Top Model* came under fire by women's groups for putting its contestants in a photo shoot that had a "murder victim" theme. Featuring models made up to look bloodied, beaten, bruised and dead, the shoot was said to glorify violence against women.

PHOTO: MARTIN VEIT

THE BEST OF BLUE
INSPIRES US

ENTERING CHINA

THE CALL OF THE EAST

Words: Miriam Rayman

H&M SHANGHAI STORE OPENING

COURTESY H&M

It's not just the luxury brands that are flocking to China. April saw the opening of H&M and C&A in Shanghai, both hoping to draw the crowds away from another recent entrant, Zara.

For most the promise of 1.3 billion consumers is too much to resist, but setting up shop in China is an arduous process and not all are successful. There is no guarantee that C&A or H&M will be able to thrive there as Zara has thus far.

James Chen, the founder of Chinese retailer UCCAL, which acts as licensee or distributor for foreign brands wanting to enter China, says, "China is a promising potential market, but it is also very difficult and competitive. There have been many international brands that were not successful."

For mid-range brands all the way up to luxury apparel brands, there are no department store chains like JCPenney or Neiman Marcus in China that could give an apparel brand an opportunity to be in 50 to 200 doors at once via a single distribution partnership. Instead, stores are essentially opened one at a time. "Department stores, as we know them in the US, do not exist in China," says Chen. "Here, they are merely 'malls' that lease out floor space to distributors or retailers like UCCAL. That distributor or retailer is then responsible for all costs ranging from the unit's construction to staff salaries."

Thus relationships with landlords are hugely important. These kinds of helpful relationships are called "guangxi" and if one does not have these kinds of contacts or close relationships with key players then doing business in China is practically impossible.

The brand's distributor is the brand manager, real estate agent and retail store operator, and a brand's success in China is heavily dependent upon this key entity and their "guangxi." In China, the distributor handles much more than a simple hand-off to a retail store chain.

Once a brand has settled on the distributor, the next thing tackled is the retail footprint. There are two main strategies for building a retail network in China.

The first is the city-by-city approach: Building up critical mass in one city before expanding to others. This is what H&M is doing there; it will open two more stores this year, focusing only on First Tier cities (Shanghai, Guangzhou and Beijing). This model is also used by the high-end brands that are keen to maximize their resources on the most attractive cities.

The second option is the approach of rolling out stores in different cities within the same region first before moving out to other regions. "We find it works best to launch the brand in Shanghai, open a few stores there and then expand out to nearby Hangzhou which is also affluent," says Chen. "That way, we can develop a more efficient regional logistics network and can take advantage of the cultural similarities amongst the consumers in the same region; that helps us to develop the product offerings."

China's retail industry is still very new and the market remains highly regionally fragmented. So while the huge geographic size does offer massive opportunities it can also create a logistical nightmare for retailers. Capturing the country's full potential would require thousands of points of sales in smaller cities.

In addition, the consumers must also be taken into account: The people are vastly different across China, in size, taste and disposable income. New emerging cities such as Tianjin, Qingdao or Shenyang are receiving lots of foreign investment so markets are set to prosper. While others such as Chongqing may look enticing with 30 million inhabitants, it centers around heavy industry and no one there is getting very rich. Says consumer researcher Paul French: "The Chongqing market is in a very low bracket. There, it's more about 30-cent instant noodles than Prada."

The climate also varies massively across China's vast land mass: The difference in winter temperatures between the north and the south is about 30 degrees Celsius and this obviously affects the apparel that is sold there.

According to Chen, the next step, building brand recognition, is where many of foreign entrants have failed. His sober message to China's current retail jamboree is this: "You need to consider the long-term potential. In our experience of launching eight brands in China, we have to build the brand recognition for two to three years before we can expand. The Chinese customer may not be aware of the international brand or be able to differentiate between real or imitation products."

ADIDAS

Branches worldwide: 410
Present in: 50+ countries
Turnover 2006: Adidas Group: $13.573 billion;
Adidas Brand: $8.917 billion

FOOTLOCKER

Stores worldwide: 3,921
Present in: North America, Europe, Australasia
Revenues 2006: $5.653 billion

GAP

Stores worldwide: 3,100+
Present in: 6 countries
Revenues 2006: $15.9 billion

H&M

Branches worldwide: 1,386
Present in: 26 countries
Turnover 2006: $11.710 billion

ZARA

Branches worldwide: 1,000 (Inditex group 3,131)
Present in: 63 countries
Turnover 2006: Inditex: $11.037 billion

JONES APPAREL

Brands owned: 30+
Present in: 60+ countries
Revenues 2006: $4.743 billion

VF CORP

Brands owned: 37
Worldwide presence
Revenues 2006: $7.033 billion

TOPSHOP

Branches worldwide: 390, with in 300 in Great Britain
Present in: 26 countries
Turnover 2006: Arcadia Group: $3.567 billion

LIZ CLAIBORNE

Stores worldwide: 339 (specialty), 336 (outlet), 625 (concession)
Worldwide presence
Revenues 2006: $4.994 billion

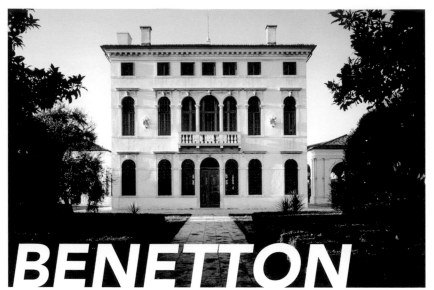

BENETTON

Branches worldwide: 5,000
Present in: 120 countries
Turnover 2006: approx. $2.575 billion

ESPRIT

Branches worldwide: 1,640 own and partner stores
(640 own, 1,000 partner)
Present in: 40 countries
Turnover 2006: Esprit Holdings Limited: $3.230 billion

MACY'S, INC.

Stores: 863 (Macy's and Bloomingdale's)
Present in: the USA
Revenues 2006: $28.711 billion
*(Formerly known as Federated Department Stores)

NIKE

Factories worldwide: 731 (as of May 2004)
Worldwide presence
Revenues 2006: $14.955 billion

LVMH

Branches worldwide: 1,800
Present in: 60 countries
Turnover 2006: $20.602 billion

NEW YORKER

Branches worldwide: 514
Present in: 17 countries
Turnover 2006: $1.346+ billion

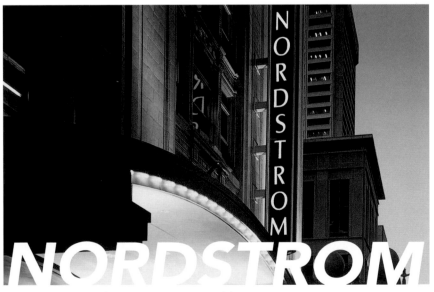

NORDSTROM

Stores: 155 (Nordstrom), 36 (Façonnable)
Present in: the USA (Nordstrom), Europe (Façonnable)
Revenues 2006: $8.561 billion

THE RICHEST

FASHION FORTUNES 2007

Words: Barbara Markert and Melanie Gropler

RANK 7, $26 BN

Bernard Arnault, LVMH

Years ago, Bernard Arnault stood in Bloomingdale's in New York and swore, "One day Dior will belong to me!" And so it came to pass. But he had hardly made himself at home at Dior when he wanted more. And so he bought and bought. Today, Arnault, with an estimated private fortune of $26 billion, is the second richest person in France–behind L'Oréal owner Liliane Bettencourt–and he heads the world's largest luxury goods conglomerate. His empire, LVMH, covers wines and spirits (Moet to Hennessy), bags (Louis Vuitton), retail (Galeries Lafayette) and fashion names such as Fendi, Donna Karan, Givenchy and Céline. Style czars such as John Galliano and Karl Lagerfeld are his employees. The group comprises more than 60 companies worldwide and it spends a million euros a year. No wonder Arnault's nicknames are "The Bill Gates of Luxury," and "Le Petit Prince de Luxe."

RANK 8, $24 BN

Amancio Ortega Gaona, Inditex group

He's the richest man of Spain: Amancio Ortega Gaona, chairman and founder of Spanish textile group Inditex. He was born in 1936 in Busdongo de Arbas, León, and moved to A Coruna at an early age. He began his textile manufacturing oper-ations in 1963. Following an initial stage of growth in the area of production, he founded Zara España, S.A. the first distribution and retailing company, three years later. The first store of the Zara chain opened on an A Coruna street in 1975. In 1985 Ortega integrated Zara in a new holding company, Industrioa de Diseno Textil, Inditex S.A. Today Inditex is one of the world's largest fashion distributors, with more than 3,100 outlets in 64 countries. In addition to Zara, the groups owns seven other commercial formats: Skhuaba, Pull and Bear, Massimo Dutti, Bershka, Stradivarius, Oysho and Zara Home.

RANK 17, $18.4 BN

Stefan Persson, H&M

The son of H&M founder Erling Persson, Stefan Persson was born in Sweden in 1947. Today he is the main shareholder of the fashion giant. Of course H&M was also born in Sweden and started out as a store called Hennes in the lakeside city of Västeras. Persson junior's career path has been dominated by the family firm–he was appointed to the board at age 32, and three years later took over the reins of the company from his father. His reign has seen H&M expand at an exponential rate. New advertising strategies were introduced, as outdoor advertising featuring famous models replaced the previously used print ads. More collections were added and the network of branches was expanded and consolidated internationally. Profits increased tenfold in the period from 1989 to 1994 alone. Persson became chairman of the supervisory board in 1998 and is still H&M's majority shareholder.

RANK 34, $14.5 BN

François-Henri Pinault, PPR

Whether François-Henri Pinault is as crafty as his father will soon be revealed, as his PPR group moves to add Puma to its stable of brands that includes Gucci, Balenciaga and McQueen. The friendly takeover of the sporting brand will be the first major test for Pinault Jr as boss of PPR. Since the transfer of power from his father in 2005, the 44-year-old's focus has mainly been on selling: this year PPR got rid of greet-ing card company Kadéos, and last year unloaded the lingerie chain Orcanta, sports retailer Made in Sport and most famously the department store Printemps and its offshoot Citadium. This separation from one of the firm's major assets, which even forms a part of the company's name Printemps-Pinault-Redoute, represented the younger Pinault's propagation of a strategy to transform of the once highly diversified retail group into a stream-lined producer of luxury goods.

*SOURCE: FORBES LIST 2007

THE MANAGERS

HANDEL LEE, RETAIL VISIONARY

Words: Miriam Rayman

New territories for China's luxury leader

Wherever there's the renovation of old buildings and the establishment of an entertainment and retail center in China, Handel Lee is sure to not be far away.

The 42-year-old American born Chinese lawyer and entrepreneur first hit the headlines with his bold initiative, Three on the Bund, in Shanghai–a five-story luxury lifestyle emporium which kick-started the renaissance of the city's once glamorous promenade, The Bund. Lee is a visionary with a passion for contemporary art at the heart of his commercial pursuits. Three on the Bund served as a grand lesson in premium lifestyle for the city's restaurateurs and bon vivants and has blazed the way for similar luxury venues to open nearby. Today the area around Three on the Bund is home to Hugo Boss, Armani, D&G, Cartier, Zegna and Shiatzy Chen, among others.

Once the Three on the Bund concept was safely established, Lee turned his magic to a set of buildings in the southeastern corner of Tiananmen Square in Beijing, a complex called Legation Quarter. There he is again creating a destination for high quality dining and retail.

That project will be complete at the end of 2007 and Lee is already excited about luxury landmark project number three: Wai Tan Yuan, to the north of the present-day Bund in Shanghai. A boutique hotel, restaurants and retail center are all planned for the site, much of which will be managed by the Rockefeller Group. Says Lee: "I'm really happy with the site because it's much more convivial than the Bund itself." The development area is a block away from the waterfront and its noisy six-lane highway. "The units are of a good size and the street network is much more suitable to high-end shopping and entertainment," says Lee.

In addition to directional new luxury fashion brands (Marni and Chloe probably will be there although the exact retail line-up is yet to be confirmed), Lee's project will include, as always, an art gallery and a interior design center.

CORPORATE 204-788-4249 Fax. 204-772-6929 USA 213-688-7602 CANADA 416-598-2545 GERMANY, AUSTRIA, TURKEY, SWITZERLAND, RUSSIA +49 7763 7021
JAPAN 81-3-5701-4621 BELGIUM +32 2 479 89 03 UK, SPAIN, FRANCE, ITALY +44 (0) 20 7428 5800 SPAIN 0034/932384661 ITALY 0039/02/57405470

1991

THE MANAGERS

MELVIN CHUA, INK PAK COMMUNICATIONS

Words: Miriam Rayman

The public relations industry is still very new in China and Ink Pak Communication Group with its prestigious fashion and lifestyle portfolio (Armani, Tod's, Hugo Boss and Valentino, among others) is leading the way.

While founder Melvin Chua was with McCann Erickson, heading its China division, he saw the gap in the market. "There wasn't much available for below the line communications," he says.

Sponsorship and PR events still are new concepts in China and the media is still very young and not very sophisticated. Which is where both the challenge and the opportunity for Chua lies. The downside is that China doesn't have that much in the way of fashion media and the professional standards of the industry aren't as high as in the Western world. But within this fluidity, there's a lot of room for maneuver. Chua can work very closely with the press, an intimacy that might be frowned upon in other more regulated media industries. He explains: "There's a lot of leeway here which allows for a close partnership."

Another great advantage of PR in China is the size of the budget that is devoted to the country. Brands are making China their main marketing focus in comparison to neighboring Taiwan, Hong Kong, Japan and Korea. This is great news in terms of events. In an attempt to consolidate budgets, the recent trend has been to stage the event in Shanghai or Beijing and then fly in regional press and dignitaries for the show. H&M's recent Asia launch event in Shanghai is a classic example.

Although Chua believes the focus on China is needed and that the country has been racing forward, he says its media and consumers still lack sophistication and an understanding of brands. "Beyond the strong leaders like Armani or LV, there's still a long way to go," he says about brand recognition and savvy consumption on the Mainland.

MICHAEL SILVER, SILVER JEANS

Words: Tim Yap

Since the launch of Silver Jeans in 1990, president Michael Silver has built up a $100 million denim company that currently distributes its Japanese and European denim-based products across North America, Europe, Asia, South America and Australia. Surprisingly, the Winnipeg, Canada-based company has only just tapped into the Benelux and the UK, but those who know Silver understand that the privately held company has always sought a quiet evolution. Today, its bottoms still have wholesale prices of $29 to $36 and Silver says he doesn't see the advantage in growing the business with new accounts. "The reality is that growth is in the verticals," he explains. "My focus is to expand within our client base."

Silver's other focus is on keeping products always in stock. "We're trying to be quicker to market," he says. Constantly adapting with the marketplace, the brand is also expanding its knit tops and secondary fabric bottom offerings. Talk to Silver, though, and one quickly realizes that the secret to his success is keeping his feet firmly planted on the ground and knowing his abilities. On launching a brand in today's marketplace, he says, "It's really, really difficult in today's world–at all price points."

That's not to say Silver hasn't tried and succeeded. In 1994, Silver and Allan Kemp launched 1921, a premium denim brand that now has double-digit growth. And in May, it unveiled Denim by Victoria Beckham, a denim line inspired by Posh. Silver explains: "She looks to us as the people who know denim."

STYLE CONSCIENCE LUXURY

billWillie

THE MANAGERS

MATTEO CAMBI, GURU

Words: Barbara Stockinger

Who's Who: What is your secret of success?

Mattteo Cambi: Research, curiosity and creativity. It's essential to be a tireless cool hunter with open eyes on the world. In my opinion to become an entrepreneur you have to be a strong observer and be ready to grasp anything interesting, innovative and avant-garde. Hence, I believe it's very important not to stop studying and traveling, to be a step ahead. Ultimately, it's crucial having a fashion designer team coming from all over the world to achieve the creative excellence typical for a melting pot.

Guru's success started in 2003 with the "marguerite" T-shirt and was initially based on guerilla marketing. How did you manage to make the brand grow?

At the beginning the economic resources were limited and the only way to promote the brand and the product was the image. I broke the classical marketing rules, experiencing a new communication model: the word of mouth, a typical viral initiative that generates a stronger buzz and it turns out to be even worthier than a classic ad. I started by having my T-shirts always with me, offering them to friends and celebs in all trendy clubs that mirrored my idea of being cool. The daisy shirt suddenly became an object of desire and young people were wearing it at all happenings.

At age 22 you founded the Jam Session Group, which owns Guru and 50% of Blue Blood today. Has it always been easy to lead that company?

It's a continuous work in progress. I like to describe myself as a creative person who is learning to become an entrepreneur.

You won a lot of prizes as a young entrepreneur. How important are these recognitions and distinctions to you?

I would say crucial, they are satisfying confirmations of the daily commitment. I firmly believe these are just the basis to achieve the excellence in every field.

A lot of brands are up-trading and launching premium lines. Is this a medium to success even for Guru?

Well... actually it's not our model. We are constantly and mainly investing in our Guru brand being our core business.

Guru already has the extension-lines Guru Shoes, G99 and Guru Gang. How important are they?

The extensions are significant to offer a proper total look and to achieve different targets, within the Guru style.

The turnover for 2006 was 90 million Euro and you expect a turnover of 100 million Euro in 2007. Being a strong and international brand, what characterizes your business?

Consolidation and investments, growth and expansion, diversification and quality, innovation and research are the ingredients of our business strategy. Today, you are allowed to be non-conformist, to surprise and to look at things under different perspectives as far as you find your own unique way. An entrepreneur needs to be dynamic, without loosing the global vision on his company and on larger scale on the world.

Describe the future of the sportswear and jeanswear market.

Stainless and at the same time in evolution. I personally believe it's decisive proposing new and sophisticated products able to interpret consumer needs and time. The communication role is vital to create a direct conversation with consumers in this contest.

What visions do you have for Guru's future?

We focus on the Guru brand by having North Europe and Far East as focal points.

PHOTO: PETER LINDBERGH

POWERED BY İSKO

İSKO
www.isko.com.tr

HEADQUARTERS

İSKO DOKUMA ISLETMELERI
SAN. VE TIC. A.S.
Organize Sanayi Bolgesi 3.Cadde
16400 Inegol Bursa TURKEY
Phone: +90 224 280 77 00
marketing@isko.com.tr

THE MANAGERS

ELYSE N. KROLL, ENK INTERNATIONAL

Words: Tim Yap

By all accounts, Elyse N. Kroll may just be the hardest working manager in the trade show business. The chief creative officer of ENK International, the US-based trade show company, she has founded such shows as The Collective, The Coterie, Accessorie Circuit, Intermezzo, Sole Commerce, Brighte Companies, Brighte Vegas, Children's Club and Blue. Today, her shows are possibly the most critical ones for both young and established brands.

Kroll began her involvement with the trade show circuit with The Collective, a show she conceived specifically for the men's contemporary market in the mid '80s. "I lived and breathed that every minute of every day for 10 years," says Kroll, whose dedication and honest, focused approach would be channeled over the next 20 years into launching seminal shows in virtually every fashion market.

And while some have suggested that her approach might be punctilious—she screens applicants meticulously while demanding their commitment to ENK shows when there are concurrent shows—her events are now respected for being "working" shows, where brands are made and orders are written. "The main purpose of a trade show," as Kroll puts it, "is to open new accounts."

"Not everyone is going to be happy," she says of the ongoing challenges of maintaining a uniform experience. "We try to make the majority happy. I think we spend probably more time than any other show company creating a good floor plan. If you have the right exhibitors, the right buyers will come. If you make it convenient for the retailers, the retailer will be happy, the exhibitors will be happy. You just always have to understand your two audiences and they each have to different needs and wants. What do the exhibitors want? They want position. What do the retailers want? They want efficiency. If you just keep your eye on the ball and figure out those two things, all the other stuff is just business problems that everyone just goes through."

These days, Kroll is leaving herself more time to focus on her role's creative aspects. Last year, ENK gained an investor, Forstmann Little & Company, the private equity firm that owns IMG. Kroll says she is enjoying the experience of having a solid infrastructure, a sounding board and some-one to share the burden of the organization with. She denies that she is going elsewhere and suggests she and the company won't stand still and are seeking new areas and locations to develop. To wit, ENK International has plans to grow its womenswear, footwear and accessories platform even larger than it already is in Las Vegas. As Kroll explains, "This is my heart and soul. I don't treat it as a business. It is what I do. We do it well. And I take care of the people who have taken care of me."

THE MANAGERS
JOS VAN TILBURG, G-STAR

Words: Lisa Dartmann

With a Raw Denim philosophy and continuity, **Jos van Tilburg** has led G-Star toward the top of the global jeans field.

Who's Who: You have made G-Star one of the most successful brands. Are you proud of your success?

Jos van Tilburg: I am proud of my team, their passion, skills and dedication.

Although ever-turbulent fashion always demands something new, you've kept your raw denim philosophy since 1996. Why?

For us it is part of G-Star's identity and therefore part of our brand foundation.

How have you managed to establish your brand over so many years?

We focus on our customer-consumer relationships and product development.

You are planning a huge store expansion all over the world; you have stepped into the US market and other projects. Why so ambitious? Why not rest on your laurels?

The world is big and we are still relatively small. It is nice to grow and to continue. G-Star needs stores in key world cities to showcase our total product offer and to function as media for the brand on the high street level.

G-Star is continually growing and is a well-organized company today. But you are not the type of person who draws a lot of attention to himself. Do you sometimes miss the creative chaos?

I'm still with my head and toes very much involved in the creative process. I love it.

G-Star makes a turnover of 470 million Euro. How do you characterize the denim business and where do you get the energy to manage the company every day?

There are many brands represented in the denim industry. That's a good thing. It pushes you to stand out from the rest and it helps keep you sharp. G-Star is a denim brand not because it's influenced by fashion. Nor do we aim to influence fashion with our denim. Denim will always remain and will never disappear from the wardrobe from each human being. It is nice to specialize in a mass-market product and treat it like a luxury item...treating denim like red wine.

Do you fear that the jeans market will slow down?

More and more men and women wear denim products and there are still so many markets to explore. Today, babies and grandparents are wearing jeans!

But do you expect that the demand for raw denim might subside?

No fear indeed as we know that raw denim is a beautiful, rich material that has endless possibilities.

And you do not worry that G-Star is no longer as sexy? Or that the tastes and brand choices of young consumers can't be predicted and that your competitors aren't sleeping?

G-Star is not a trend-led brand and our target group varies from 15- to 45-years-old, which is a wider bandwidth than most jeans brands. Remaining sexy is about attitude; we must retain the right attitude.

Every month G-Star delivers new articles to its stores. Is that the key to your success? Or do you sometimes wonder if you are you overloading the market?

We try to offer the market what it needs. Fresh updates in store; it's part of today's zap culture. We are proud that we can deliver new styles on a regular basis. It keeps it exciting for us as developers but certainly also for our retailers and consumers.

For years, the highly conceptual G-Star fashion show has been a huge hit with audiences. Is there a danger that one year it might be boring? And if so, how do you deal with that?

We are always afraid it will get boring. But we are not afraid to deal with this challenge and pressure.

G-Star is established as an international brand. In which areas can you grow further?

There is continuous growth by evolving steadily.

What are your secrets of success besides innovation and speed fashion?

We are innovative product developers and are not developing speed fashion. We carefully create products that we hope our consumers recognize as tomorrow's classics.

What are your plans for the American market and the rest of the world?

To continuously work on new product developments.

What other visions do you have in your mind?

Do you have another few hours?

You have so many years in the jeans business. Why does it still fascinate you?

More and more opportunities arise in different areas: In product material possibilities, ecological products, unexplored markets.... Denim is simply the most worn type of product worldwide through all layers of society. If you realize that deeply, well, you can't be anything else but fascinated.

Follow us...
through the *Magic World* of
VICTOR'S woven tapes

V...as *Variety*

THE MANAGERS

KARL-HEINZ MÜLLER, BREAD & BUTTER

Words: Lisa Dartmann

With his progressive trade show concept, Bread&butter's **Karl-Heinz Müller** has turned the fashion-fair business on its ear.

Who's Who: With your "trade show" concept replacing the traditional trade fair, you have turned the entire industry inside out. Are you proud of your success?

Karl-Heinz Müller: I have to hesitate there–pride goes before a fall! Our success wasn't pulled out of a hat, the concept was developed over a period of years–primarily through a dialog with exhibitors and visitors. I am very happy with how this development has turned out. The job we have done is gaining recognition and is widely supported.

Isn't it somewhat strenuous to keep coming up with new ideas?

Every day presents a new challenge. We never rest on our laurels, we are too busy always trying to keep pace with this every-changing industry. We don't define ourselves in terms of the masses; we are aligned with visionary, creative people who identify with us. These relationships can be very productive.

How have you managed to keep Bread&butter as a brand on a firm footing from one year to the next?

We are never satisfied–we're hungry, and fresh enough to be always on the go. I don't stay chained to a desk. I prefer to be out and about, meeting people from all kinds of different cultures and scenes–art, music, events, and so on. We are enormously responsive to the needs of our interest groups, so there is always something new going on and our product stays young and fresh.

And where do get your ideas?

New ideas can come from anywhere. Just recently a textile agent contacted me about booking a stand in Barcelona, and I thought why not? Denim weavers, outfitters and washers are also part of the community that meets here, and they want to get a look at how their product turns out. I'm planning an upcoming brainstorming session with sourcing specialists. Who knows what will come out of that?

The plans you come up with are always presenting the industry with new and astounding surprises. What do you enjoy so much about this particular challenge?

It's a question of your mentality. As a typical Aquarius I revel in constant change–it's not just about making money, I really do just enjoy making things happen. We have a staff of 100 who are all straining at the leash. It's impossible to drag your heels.

Where do you get the energy for all these new concepts?

I really don't know. I feel young at heart still, and constantly driven. My company pretty much represents an extended family for me, but I increasingly want to take a step back and have more time for myself.

Do you ever fear losing your edge and running out of ideas?

Of course it is tiring to have to be so switched on all the time, like at my 50th birthday party–there were 500 people there and I couldn't even say hello to everybody. I don't want to move in exalted circles; I would find that quite awful. My door is open for everybody from CEOs to interns.

And you have no concerns about losing your credibility or becoming vulnerable in the industry?

All pioneers are vulnerable. I don't like this atmosphere of constant kvetching. A lot of international competitors can't bring themselves just to say, "Wow, man, you have some great ideas." They have to find a fly in the ointment. I have gradually learned not to go peddling my ideas. Rather, you have to first develop a solid concept, check that it is plausible, and then go public with it. I used to be much quicker off the mark.

The first Fashion Week Berlin is already on the drawing boards.

What's your general view of how Berlin is developing as a fashion center?

Berlin is an ideal platform for showrooms and cool young brands and off-show trade fairs. But it can't yet measure up to the international fashion metropolises. The planned Fashion Week Berlin seems like a soulless, anonymous event.

How are the plans for Fashion Week in Barcelona coming along?

There is a lot of talk about a Fashion Week and we have let ourselves be caught up in it. Rather than artificially stretching the Bread&butter out, we want to really shake up the town for the three-day period. Our priority is on enhancing quality. Nor are we interested in hosting large-scale vertical exhibitors in Barcelona. We would rather concentrate on those segments which fit with our concept.

What visions have you yet to reveal?

We want to carry on working on content and make improvements in a few areas. For instance, the congestion in the entrance area, the inadequate number of restaurants and other practical requirements such as the number of toilets "more nice and clean." It is essential to keep on improving and adding to what we already have. There is a lot of potential still to be tapped in Barcelona.

You have been in the business for a considerable time. What do you find so fascinating about it?

I just like the industry. It's the people that I find particularly fascinating. There are some really great people in the fashion world who are doing some amazing things.

The art of Denim

DENIM

MARCHING ON

After several seasons of high priced so-called premium denim, it is now the time for super trendy yet affordable jeans. Prominent new names are Dr. Denim Jeansmakers, Cheap Monday and Produkt Homme. They all come from Scandinavia and are making major waves in the market.

PRODUKT HOMME

DR. DENIM JEANSMAKERS

073

Those who want to stick to well-known designer names or premium denim brands have more options than ever. Famous designers such as Karl Lagerfeld, Alexander McQueen and John Galliano started their denim lines to please clotheshorses and brand-addicts; at the same time more US and Australian premium denim brands such as Habitual, Bread Denim, J Brand and 18th Amendment have hit the scene with high quality fabrics and fits.

HABITUAL

ALEXANDER McQUEEN

Salsa
FITS MY LIFE

STREET

URBAN RENEWAL

Streetwear is having a renaissance. Rather than offering typical slouchy urban styles, it now often features a cool designer-like touches. 55DSL, Henrik Vibskov, WoodWood, Björkvin, Converse by John Varvatos, Triple Five Soul and Umbro by Kim Jones are among the brands spearheading this new movement.

HENRIK VIBSKOV

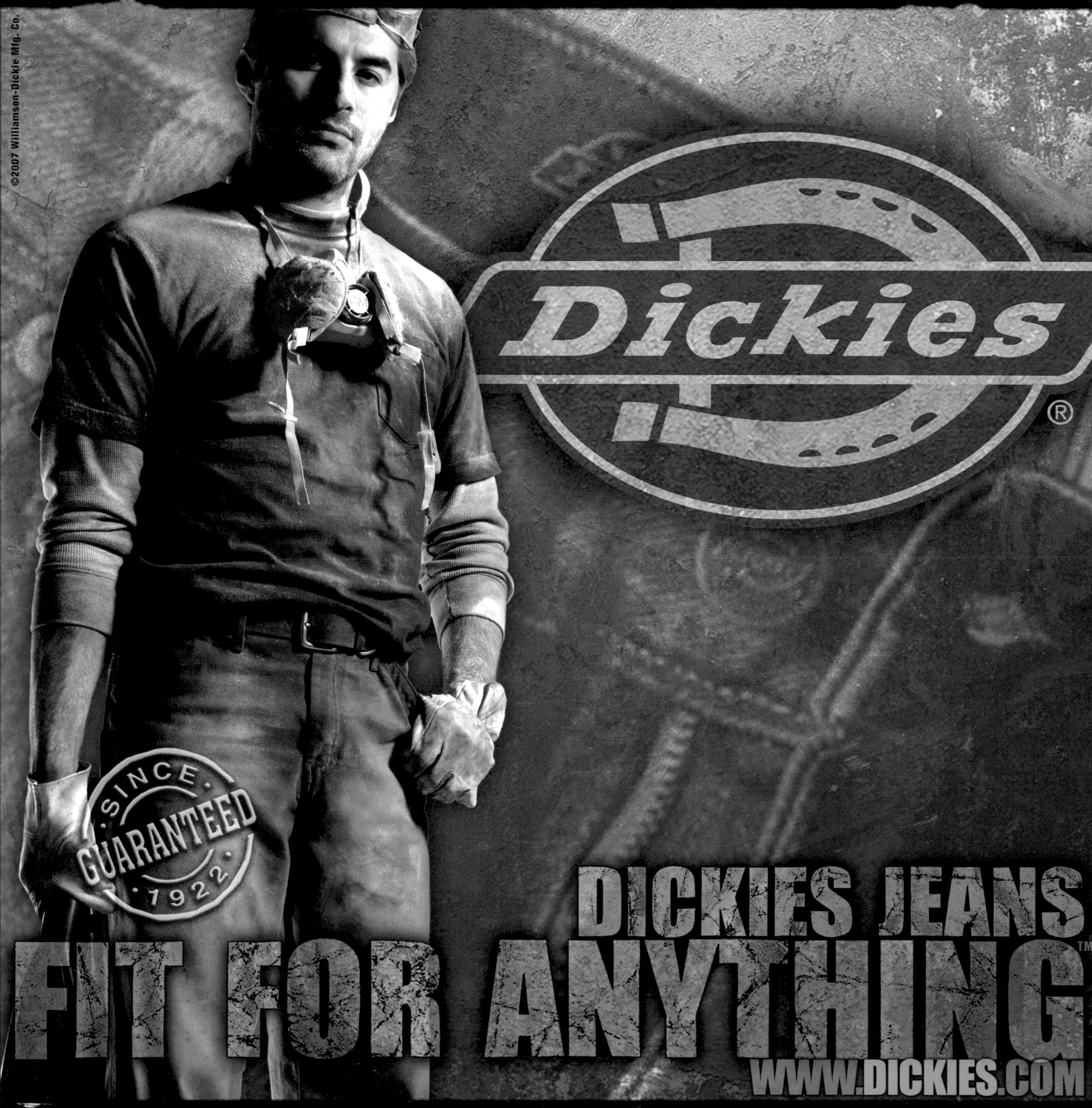

Dickies®

SINCE
GUARANTEED
1922

DICKIES JEANS
FIT FOR ANYTHING™

SPORTS

SEARCH FOR TESTIMONIALS

Performance sports brands recognized the trend and are no longer sticking to traditional marketing techniques. What goes for fashion also goes for them—a little bit of glamour can help attract attention.

Recently more prominent (sports) faces have turned out to be prominent testimonials for sporty labels: Rbk counts on football star Thierry Henry, Adidas promotes its qualities with well-known sport stars such as

footballer/fashion icon David Beckham. German brand Falke also recently hopped on the train with a rather risky engagement. It sponsored former boxing championship Henry Maske for his final-final

revenge fight against Virgil Hill. After his ten-year absence from the boxing ring nobody really believed in Maske's comeback. But in a Rocky Balboa-esque way Maske won-and so did Falke.

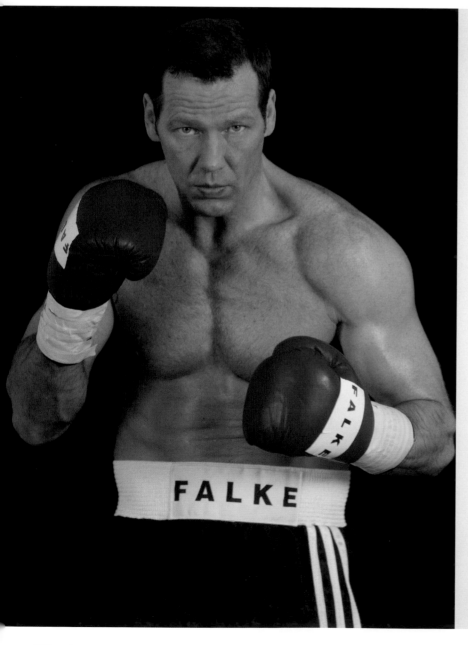

MARCO ZAMORA

NEW LUXE/DIRECTIONAL
U.S. PRIME

It's a land that loves new things, so lucky for it–and the world–the USA is currently home to a bumper crop of fresh designers and new luxe brands. Newbies generating the most buzz this year include The Smooth Company, Samantha Pleet, B.Son, Nicholas K, Corpus, Spurr and Robert Geller.

Denimhead®

Trend Forecast Service
for Denim &
Casual Sportswear

www.denimhead.com

BOOMTOWNS

Shanghai is China's richest city but average income is only US$300.

Still, urban incomes in China rose last year by 9.6% and McKinsey predicts that lower middle class Chinese will make up 44% of the urban population by 2011 with a total spending power of 4.8 trillion Chinese Yuan.

Shanghai's total mall retail space is 2.5 million sq. meters (26.9 million sq. feet).

Shanghai's retail sales are growing at around 12% a year.

China ranks third in terms of retail sales, behind the United States and Japan.

Although China joined the World Trade Organization in 2001, the US government estimates that 20% of its production is still dedicated to counterfeit goods.

China's 492-meter-high, Shanghai World Financial Tower will be the tallest building in the world when it opens in 2008.

The world's fourth largest city and Latin America's biggest, Sao Paolo is Brazil's main gateway for foreigners, the country's richest city and a cultural pinnacle. Its area covers 1,509 square kilometers (583 sq. miles) and it has a population of 10,406,66. According to ABIT, the Brazilian Textile and Clothing Industry Association, the fashion sector comprises more than 30,000 companies and employs approximately 1.5 million Brazilian workers. In addition, the Brazilian textile segment aims at recovering its 1% share of the world market, which is equivalent to increasing the volume of exports up to US $4 billion per year by 2008. There are more than 50 fashion fairs and shows in Brazil each year.

FASANO

SPFW
SÃO PAULO FASHION WEEK

002568

SPFW INVERNO 07
CARBON FREE

With 1,081 sq. kilometers (417 sq. miles) of space, Moscow is Russia's capital and its largest city. About 10.5 million people, or about 7% of the entire Russian population, live there. This also makes Moscow Europe's most populous city.

Although the birth rate has risen, the average age of Moscow's population continues to increase. In 2004 there were more than twice as many people over the age of 55 as there were under the age of 14. The average monthly salary is about $400 so the standard of living in Moscow is not very high–especially since it was ranked as the world's most expensive city by Mercer Human Resource Consulting's 2006 World Cost of Living Survey.

However, Moscow is one of the top cities in the world for billionaires. *Forbes* ranked it second in the highest number of billionaires, sur-passed only by New York. In 2004, Russia's 36 billionaires (of whom only three did not live in Moscow) held the equivalent of 24% of the country's GDM. The nouveau-riche, who are disparangingly called "New Russians," flaunt their wealth in the city's posh stores and clubs. Moscow is slowly establishing itself as one of the Eastern fashion capitals with fairs taking place there such as Jeans, Ispo Russia and CPM.

ADMFLEX ®

STRETCH DENIM WITH CORE SPUN T400

FOR THAT
LASTING
FIT!

Mumbai, which was called Bombay until 1996, has a population of about 18 million, with a density of about 29,000 persons per square kilometer. Therefore Mumbai is considered the most populous city of India. By 2020 it is likely to be the most populous city in the world with an estimated 28.5 million residents. The city is the commercial and entertainment capital of India and home to its "Bollywood" film industry. It also houses important financial institutions such as the National Stock Exchange of India and many headquarters of Indian companies. Mumbai has attracted migrants from all over India because of the immense business opportunities and the relatively high standard of living. Mumbai contributes 10% of all factory employment, 40% of all income tax colllections and 40% of India's foreign trade. Until the 1980s, Mumbai owed its prosperity largely to textile mills and clothing production but the local economy has since been diversified to include engineering and information technology. The middle class in Mumbai drives of the city's consumer boom. Upward mobility among Mumbaikars has led to a direct increase in consumer spending.

GBMI®

EIGHT WORLD CLASS BRANDS.
LIMITLESS DESIGNS.
ONE COMPANY.

DIESEL   NOMASS   SEAN JOHN   DRYSHOD   MEHANDI   NAUTICA   MECCA   7 FOR ALL MANKIND FOOTWEAR

6500 HOLLISTER AVENUE, SANTA BARBARA, CALIFORNIA 93117 USA • P 805.562.5600 • F 805-562-5620 • www.gbmi.net

THE BIG ONE

BREAD&BUTTER, BARCELONA

The decision to have just one Bread&butter worked out well for its organizers: the January 2007 Barcelona edition attracted almost 83,000 visitors from 109 countries during its three-day run. For its July 2007 edition, B&b expects at least the same number of visitors, plus an impressive number of approximately 1,000 brands that will present their summer collections in the various streetwear, jeanswear and fashion segments.

Although it was born in Berlin, it's clear that this whopper of a show has really found its calling in sunny Spain. Expect it to continue to draw in the crowds there.

091

THE NEWCOMERS

UNITED
LAS VEGAS

With MAGIC taking up numerous halls of the Las Vegas Convention Center, Project in three parts of the Sands, Pool in a parking lot and other smaller shows elsewhere, one might think the last thing Vegas needed was another trade show. But Ryan Walker thought it did. So he launched United in February. Laid-back and featuring just a few dozen independent brands, the small show was such a hit that it is returning in August—and launching a New York edition in July. In the ongoing US trade show saga, Walker is the latest to play David. Some Davids and their shows have been squashed; others became Goliaths themselves. It will be interestesing to see how Walker fares....

FASHION WEEK *BERLIN*

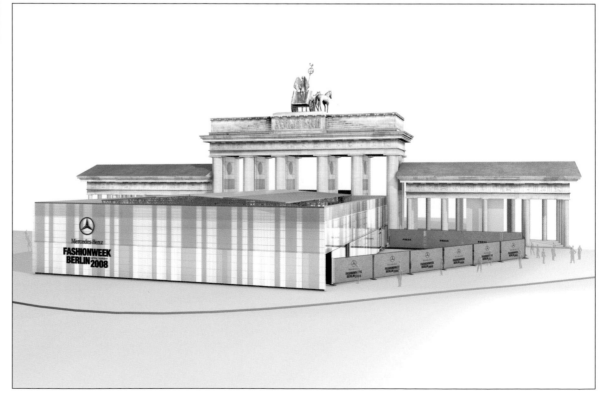

Streetwear leaves, designers arrive: although Berlin no longer hosts a Bread & butter show, the German capital has gotten a rather fashionable replacement. In July 2007 the first Fashion Week Berlin will take place and present several designer catwalk shows. So far Boss, Michael Michalsky, Rudolf Dassler by Puma, Anglomania by Viviennne Westwood and German newcomer designers such as Kaviar Gauche, Talkingmeanstrouble and C.Neeon will show their collections in a tent at the Brandenburg Gate. International agency IMG is behind the organization and realization of the Fashion Week that is primarily sponsored by Mercedes-Benz.

Witness the strength of street this August.

MAGIC delivers the most comprehensive selection of emerging and established brands in the business. MAGIC is where the fashion industry's strongest players come to compete.

Join us, August 27 – 30, 2007
Las Vegas Convention Center
www.MAGIConline.com

IQONS

THE STYLE NETWORK

Words: Emma Holmqvist

Iqons (www.iqons.com), the international online community for fashion folks of all denominations, is growing. Since launching during London Fashion Week in February 2007, the site has attracted more than 10,000 members and the number is constantly on the up.

It's no wonder that Iqons has proven to be such a hit: in essence, it is a MySpace or YouTube exclusively for fashion mavens. Sandra Backlund, a Swedish fashion designer, was one of the first members to benefit from the worldwide exposure that Iqons generates. Recently Backlund landed the first prize in fashion design at the April 2007 edition of Hyères International Festival of Fashion and Photography. "I did join Iqons when it was still in its newborn phase, but it was not long until I noticed what a great platform it is for global meet-ings and marketing within fashion. You can spread your work and in-crease your contacts internationally in a way that is almost impossible in real life, especially if you are based outside of the traditional fashion cities like I am," she enthuses.

What sets Iqons apart from the likes of MySpace–the site that revolutionized online networking–is that it targets people in the fashion industry only, whereas MySpace is for people from all professions and interests. Another point of difference is that Iqons puts much emphasis on forming professional relationships while MySpace encourages personal friendships. However, it still provides an excellent platform for fledging musicians, artists and filmmakers. Still, the social aspects are important and flirting and dating are still in the cards on both Iqons and MySpace. This becomes obvious when one realizes that most Iqons members state their sexual orientation and relationship status. In terms of the prevailing age group, MySpace and Iqons seem to attract similar members: under 35s dominate, but people of all ages sign up. This younger majority is probably due to the fact that this age group consists of confident Internet users who are keen to build their careers and find new friends or lovers.

Since the aim behind the initiative is to provide a platform where fashion professionals mingle and establish a point of contact, the service is free; just like in the world of magazines, the project is largely funded by advertising.

Apart from offering an excellent networking system, Iqons allows its members to flaunt their talent, share their passion or wisdom, rate

STYLE BLOGGER DIANE PERNET'S IQONS PAGE

fashion shows, view video clips, get to know other users and search for potential employers or employees. The site offers many exciting initiatives such as creative competitions and guest appearances by fashion heavyweights. These so-called "Featured Iqons" comment and issue advice to a select crew of members each month. Mostly these members are fashion designers, but people from other fashion disciplines are welcome to have their work constructively criticized too. So far, Featured Iqons have included Vivienne Westwood, Alber Elbaz and *Vogue Italia* editor in chief Franca Sozzani. John Galliano has also agreed to be one soon.

The best thing about this initiative, says Suran Goonatilake, who co-founded the site with creative director Rafael Jimenez, is that it "creates a dialogue between Iqons members and established fashion players." And it is not only the new designers who are the winners, he stresses: "Big, established names are always on the lookout for fresh talent and this provides them with a good opportunity to find suitable candidates."

Keeping with the democratic nature of the site, direct feedback from users is encouraged. Iqons is constantly being updated and new features are constantly launched on the site. With an entire global fashion community to support and entertain, it is no mean feat keeping them busy.

DIGITAL CHINA

COURTING CHINA'S WIRED-UP YOUTH

Words: Miriam Rayman

Twenty years ago there were no shopping malls in China. Now Shanghai alone has 50. Growing accustomed to this rate of change has resulted in a group of Chinese young people who are extremely reliant on fresh stimulation. And today marketers there are realizing that the best way to reach them is through online campaigns.

Chinese urban kids grew up with the screen. Be it mobile, out of home or on the bedroom desktop, their engagement with new media is much more intense than equivalent demographics overseas. The traditional media industry is still very young in China and the Internet has been around for as long and in some cases longer than established communication channels in the West. For example, the fashion page on popular website www.sina.com was launched long before spring 2005 when *Vogue* first hit Chinese newsstands.

The Chinese fashionista will head to traditional media such as magazines and TV shows to get the updates but knows that mass media is talking to a very broad demogra-

phic. Says PT Black of Jigsaw International research agency: "Broadcast media is very general and talks to the lowest common denominator so it doesn't really convey much opinion." Because of that, he concludes, "The Chinese kid needs to go online."

The online world also provides a new space where Chinese youth can express themselves more freely than in the convention-bound reality. Blogs

NIKE

and online forums provide a vital support system and violent computer games are incredibly popular (online users have risen to 137 million in China, just behind the 210 million US users.)

With self expression so new, Chinese cities do not really have many social venues such as community centers or music hangouts so the virtual arena is the ideal place to come together and gain access

to other like-minded people. Says Black: "The Internet is vital for connecting those trends together."

In addition, any child born after the Cultural Revolution has only experienced economic growth and political stability–pure optimism. But Nick Barham, strategic planning director at Wieden and Kennedy, says, "Just because people feel good, doesn't mean that they have no critical judgment, nor that they will be convinced by clichéd images of the good life." When Wieden and Kennedy worked with Nike on the 2005 Just Do It campaign, it was very keen to break the sickly sweet trend in Chinese advertising which presents everything as shiny and glossy using beautiful, smiling celebrities. So it gave Chinese kids hand-held cameras and got them to contribute to the campaign.

It all centered around the Nike website where kids were encouraged to make, watch and vote on five-minute documentaries. Says Nike China's brand communications director Ed Elworthy: "We knew online was the way to do it–digital is the prime medium for us in China."

GOOD NOSE FOR TRENDS

TRY THE FIRST AND REAL MATT FROSTED COMING SOON... ★ ★ ★ ★ ★

Mod Amont Paris
18 - 21 September `07

MADEIRA

IDEAS
TRANSFORMED
INTO
THREADS...

design the future
MADEIRA

MADEIRA Rudolf Schmidt KG - Zinkmattenstr. 38 - D-79108 Freiburg - Tel: +49 (0)761-510400
Fax: +49 (0)761-508456 - Homepage: www.madeira.com - eMail: service@madeira.de

SECOND LIFE

ONLINE RETAILING'S LATEST WAVE

Words: Max Padilla

Innovative brands are finding new and unique ways to advertise on the Internet beyond relying on viral efforts from blogs and My-Space. One unusual method to promote product is on Second Life (www.secondlife.com), an interactive online 3-D "virtual world" where enthusiasts create avatars—virtual selves—to interact with other users from around the world. After downloading the software, the Second Life process starts with creating an identity around a pseudonym. Then one selects an avatar from an initial assortment of options from chic city dwellers to Harajuku girls. After picking his or her eye color and hairstyle there is also an opportunity to outfit the avatar with innerwear such as shorts and T-shirts. One can then enter the virtual world with some of his or her real-world style intact.

With nearly 6 million users, the draw of Second Life is based on interacting and chatting with other Lifers, in experiences ranging from tame—such as dancing—to frequenting an array of seedy strip clubs. There's also an economy with virtual Linden "dollars" (available with a paid membership; Linden Lab is the company behind Second Life) that can be used for buying everything from land to boxer briefs. This premise excites brands and businesses that are interested in reaching out to the site's desirable young demographic, cited with an average age of 32.

In summer 2006, American Apparel became the first "real life" company to open a shop in Second Life and got a flurry of press from *The Times of London* to *The New York Times* to *Time* magazine. "The Second Life shop was purely a marketing experiment," says American Apparel's web director Raz Schionning. "The big benefit for us was in the publicity surrounding it. We were then followed by an awful lot of companies like Starwood Hotels and Toyota."

Opening a store on Second Life mirrors a real one with hefty set-up costs and rent. But the virtual store can also move goods along with promoting new merchandise. Second Life also monitors the shop's traffic. The virtual American Apparel store resembles a real-life store but the setting is more exotic—on an island called Lerappa ("apparel" spelled backwards). The 65,536-sq.-meter (705,424-sq.-foot) two-story shop resembles one of the LA-based vertical's stores in Japan. American Apparel inaugurated its Lerappa location with a virtual opening party playing music from the store's Viva Radio concept and offering free beer and discounts. Inside the store one can buy clothes for his or her avatar from items in American Apparel's basic collection with Linden money.

Reebok also opened a Second Life Rbk store that resembles a high concept standalone with rap music, plasma screens and a music playlist. Avatars can customize a pair of Reebok Custom DJII "blanks" in a five-step process. In the Adidas virtual shop, Adidas tracksuit-clad avatars test out the a3 Microride shoe and can purchase footwear at a fraction of its real-life cost. The German sportswear giant timed its virtual campaign to coincide with the real world a3 Microride one, a design perfect for Second Lifers with its bounciness.

In Second Life's world there are also malls and shopping centers featuring multibrand stores such as Release, which sells black Adidas shell toes for $300 Linden dollars, alongside comic books and baseball bats. Its neighbor Delta sells camouflage clothes and Second Lifers can chat with owner Paco. There's also Ubercrummy & Kitsch, a parody of that ubiquitous lifestyle chain that sells message tees and body-conscious underwear to a male clientele. Unfortunately on Second Life there is a proliferation of stores that sell tattoos, piercings and nipple shields. Remember that the site is only a representation of its users. So until Marc Jacobs creates an avatar don't expect any cool designer duds.

Second Life is the brainchild of a San Francisco-based tech company called Linden Lab. The Linden dollar's value to the US dollar fluctuates in its exchange as much as the greenback does with the Euro, which can cause as much of a headache for virtual retailers as its does in the real world.

VIRTUAL AMERICAN APPAREL STORE

jbs

MENS UNDERWEAR

LONGCHAMPNEW YORK

WISHATLANTA

what you
want is
what you
can get.
unite
youniverse!

Cross Jeanswear Co. cROSs crossjeans.com

THE SHOP AT BLUEBIRD LONDON

GURU

PRESENTS
THE EDGE OF
DARKNESS
A BEAUTIFUL MYSTERY
WWW.GURU.IT
PHOTOGRAPHY BY JENNY HANDS

SLAM JAM
MILAN

COLIN S®
jeanswear

www.colins.com.tr

GIORGIO ARMANI & RUSSELL CROWE

TEAMING UP

In March 2006 Academy Award-winning actor Russell Crowe and a business partner purchased a 75% stake in Australia's South Sydney Rabbitohs National Rugby League Club. Soon after, Crowe asked his friend Giorgio Armani to design special suits for the players. Here, Armani speaks about this unique project and the challenges he faced making clothes for latter-day Aussie gladiators.

Who's Who: When were you first approached to complete this project?

Giorgio Armani: A little over a year ago my friend Russell Crowe called and said he had a proposition for me. He doesn't call often and when he does it is usually about something very important. "Hi, Giorgio, I need an outfit for the Academy Awards, what do you suggest?" Or, "Hey, I'm getting married, what should I wear?" Or, in this case, "I've bought a share in the Rabbitohs and they are going back to the top of the premiership,

would you help to design a special outfit for them?"

What attracted you to completing this project?

Well first and foremost, Russell is a great friend, so I wanted to help him out. Russell always comes up with unique ideas. He tells me that it is an Australian cultural phenomenon to cheer for the outsider. That cheering for the underdog is an Italian trait too; perhaps it is global. Secondly I love sport of all kinds, and love to dress sportsmen and athletes. They are like modern day gladiators; and because they have to show real dedication and skill they are an inspiration for all of us.

Have you ever seen a Rugby League game?

No I haven't, but I have watched rugby league on television–it is the variety of the game we have here in Italy. Mauro and Mirko Bergamasco, who play for the national side, often come to my shows, and I am friends with England's World Cup–winning captain, Lawrence Dallaglio. He has also been to my shows in Milan, and chose a Giorgio Armani suit for his wedding last July. After this collaboration, I will be sure to watch their games now, even if only on TV.

What did Russell Crowe tell you about the game and his team?

Russell basically said that he'd bought into his favorite Australian rugby league team and wanted to take them back to the top of the league. He wanted to fill them with confidence and thought that a good starting point would be for them to

arrive at matches looking great and standing tall in Armani. He told me as a Rabbitoh's fan, it's not the losing that hurts, it's the hope that will kill you. He also told me of the diversity within the clubhouse, how South's embrace all races and backgrounds. To be quite frank, he told me the whole and complete history of the team. He is very persuasive.

How do you approach creating a uniform for a sports team?

The object of a team uniform is to give the players something that they want to wear and that makes them feel good. For the England football team, I decided to reflect the fact that this was a young dynamic squad, with several players who were really fashion literate–so I created the Beckham jacket, an unstructured jacket which was very body-conscious. For the Rabbitohs, I realized that I was dealing with men who are powerfully built and so need something a bit more softly tailored. The final outfit is therefore based on an Giorgio Armani soft tailored two-button custom fit suit and looks extremely smart and slick. There was something that appealed to me in the playful paradox of extremely tough men dressed in a super-sharp urban outfit–as though they are saying, we are perfectionists, in dress and in rugby: look out! Nobody else will dress like this in this season of Rugby League. Russell knows I enjoy breaking new ground. I also liked that he wanted to embrace a complex history through the crest design with dignity and a sense of humor.

Have you outfitted other football teams?

Never rugby teams but I have dressed many football teams. I was,

I believe, the first designer to really identify football players as potential style icons. I dressed the Italian team for Italia '90–the World Cup–and then put David James, then Liverpool's goalkeeper, on the catwalk in 1995. David also appeared in an Armani Jeans advertising campaign. Since then I have dressed the Chelsea team and many great players like Ronaldo, Luis Figo, Fabio Cannavaro and Andriy Shevchenko. In fact, I have opened a store in Andriy's hometown of Kiev in the Ukraine, and he is currently the face of Armani Collezioni. I really love football–I am, after all, Italian.

What are the challenges and rewards of outfitting athletes?

The challenges are the result of their physical development–muscles are large, and thighs and arms in particular can be more substantial than normal. That is why it is best to go with a custom fit approach, where garments can be individually tailored to each player. The rewards are in seeing your clothes worn by great role models. We are used to seeing actors and musicians wear designers' creations, but I believe that sportsmen have just as much influence, if not more so, than those in the entertainment industry–especially where men are concerned. Athletes have that modern day gladiator aspect, though I have to observe that no other team I have dressed plays a sport so fitting that description.

What have you learned about the team to complete this project?

I have learnt that Rugby League players have the thickest legs and largest feet of any athlete's in my experience to date!

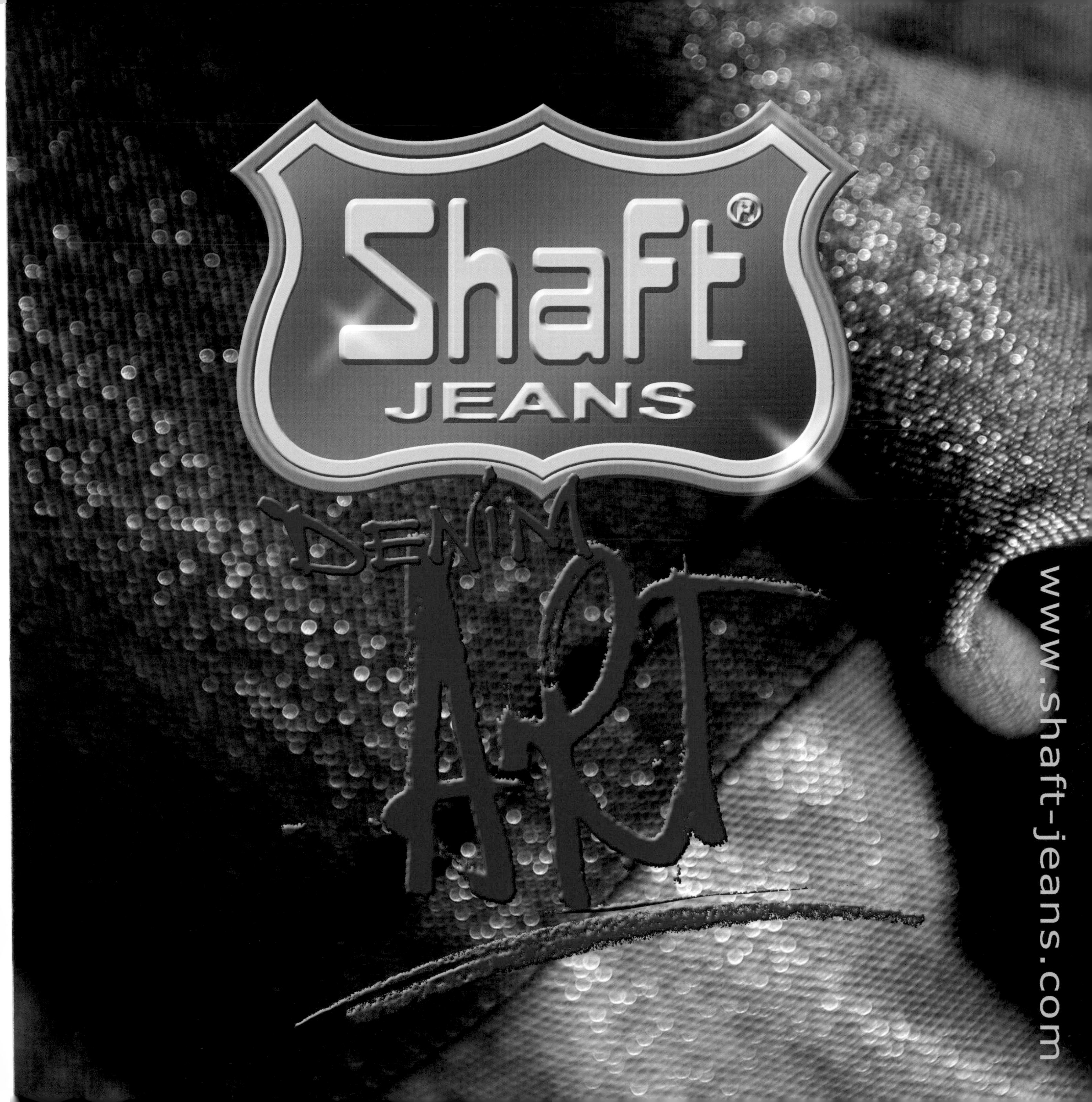
Shaft®
JEANS
DENIM
ART
www.shaft-jeans.com

ELECTRIC COLORS

DRESS: KSUBI
TANK TOP: HARD TAIL

PHOTO: ERIK SWAIN

134

ASR September 7–9, 2007
San Diego Convention Center, San Diego, CA

Register Today!
To register, visit www.ASRbiz.com

ASR September

Over 500 brands and 1200 booths showcasing the hottest men's, juniors and kid's Spring 08 fashions, from the most widely recognized surf, skate, swim, snow, moto and fashion manufacturers

Efficiently and effectively accomplish months of coordination, prospecting, line-showings and meetings in an energetic yet professional 3-day forum

FREE seminars to enhance your business needs

View the newest Spring 08 trends at the ASR Runway show, co-sponsored by

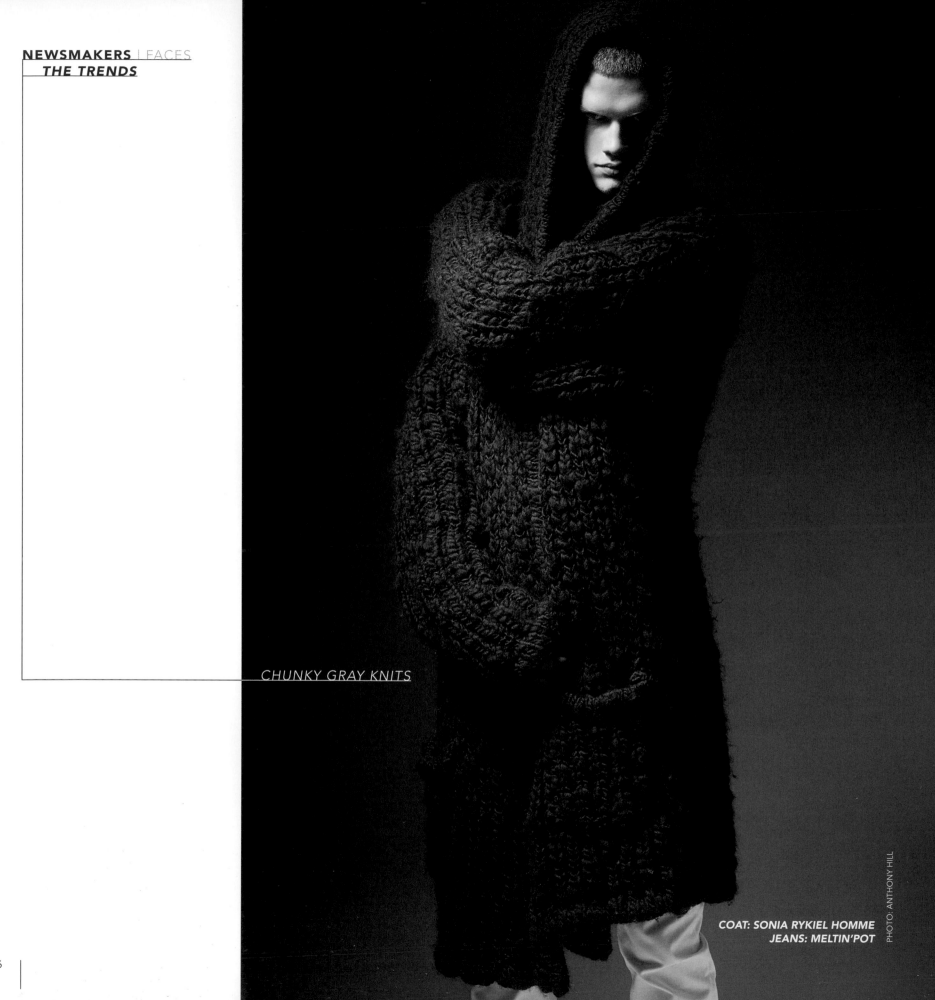

CHUNKY GRAY KNITS

COAT: SONIA RYKIEL HOMME
JEANS: MELTIN'POT

PHOTO: ANTHONY HILL

dioNisO

BACK TO
THE FUTURE

dioNisO

tel Showroom +39 02 55190119
www.dioniso.net

NEW SILHOUETTES

C. P. COMPANY

TURBANS

SHOE' SHI BAR (LOOKBOOK)

DRDENIM JEANSMAKERS®

A good pair of jeans is like a member of the family
www.drdenimjeans.com

NEOSENS IS THE NEW WAY OF APPRECIATING QUALITY

Made in Spain - T> +34 941 40 33 61 - www.neosens.com

neosens®

Alta Expresión

Tradition & Avant-garde
Opera & Rock n'Roll
"Crianza & Gran Reserva"
High Tech & Craftsmanship
Heart & Reason

All from La Rioja!

NIGHT & DAY
MEN & WOMEN

BRAY STEVE ALAN®

PART TWO
FACES

INTRODUCTION

A FAMILY AFFAIR

One dictionary definition of the word "family" is "a group of people united by certain convictions or a common affiliation." In other words, just sharing the same genes doesn't necessarily make a family. In the fashion world, making the same jeans can also create a kinship. On the following pages, meet 26 of sportswear's "first families" who were shot over a period of more than two months by photographer Marco La Conte. Some are related by blood while others are bonded by business.

FOR FULL CREDITS PLEASE SEE PAGE 226

Earnest Sewn
March 8, New York City, USA

Evisu
March 13, New York City, USA

Evisu
March 13, New York City, USA

Guess
March 22, Los Angeles, USA

Goldsign
March 27, Los Angeles, USA

Levi's
March 28, San Francisco, USA

True Religion
March 29, Los Angeles, USA

Blue Holdings
March 30, Pacific Palisades, California, USA

Meltin'Pot
April 11, Matino, Lecce, Italy

Sixty
April 16, Rome, Italy

Ben Sherman
April 23, London, UK

Jack&Jones
April 30, Brande, Denmark

THE SHOOT
A FAMILY AFFAIR

PHOTOGRAPHER:
Marco La Conte,
www.marcolaconte.com

Photo Assistants to
Marco La Conte:
USA
NYC: Chad Murray;
LA/San Francisco: Andrew Paul Bonenfant
Europe
Franco Bello
Except Fornari/Diesel/Rifle:
Simone Zoeggeler

HAIR/MAKE UP:
Diane da Silva using Shu Uemura, www.
dasilvamakeup.com (Earnest Sewn, True
Religion and Blue Holdings),
Chantal van Gogh / b creatives (Blue
Blood), Carol Morley@frank agency (Ben
Sherman, Lee Cooper, Firetrap)

7 FOR ALL MANKIND
March 29, Los Angeles, USA

Left to right:
Rick Crane / Executive Vice President of
Sales and Merchandising, Mike Egeck
/ Chief Executive Officer, Peter Koral /
President and Chairman, Liz Hampshire /
Chief Operations Manager, Tim Kaeding
/ Vice President of Design & Creative
Director.

Location: 7 For All Mankind
headquarters.

BEN SHERMAN
April 23, London, UK

Miles Gray, Ben Sherman's CEO, said he
declined to pose for this portrait to draw
more attention to the rest of the Ben
Sherman family.

Left to right:
Martin Morris / Head of Graphics &
Interiors, James Bettle / International
Sales Director, Mark Maidment / Creative
Director, Michelle Bartz / Womenswear
Global Brand Manager, Jamie Hall / Global
Marketing Manager.

Location: Ben Sherman showroom.

BLUE BLOOD
April 18, Amsterdam,
The Netherlands

1st row, left to right:
Sule Orhan / Store staff, Gregor Jaspers /
Retail Manager, Lee Stuart / Store staff.
2nd row
Alex Jaspers / Sales Director, Cressida
Wilcox / Womenswear Designer, Mandy
Meuwese / PR Manager.
3rd row
Bas Hoeve / After Sales Manager,
Jomima Leiwahabessy / Fashion Assistant,
Steve te Pas / CEO.
4th row
Dave Steijn / Finance Administrator.
5th row
Oktay Ozkan / Sales Representative,
Jason Denham / Creative Director.
6th row
Edward van Loo / Operations Manager,
Evelyne Vernge / Store staff, Rabin Basu /
Store Manager.
7th row
Ali Kirby / Graphic Designer, Barbera van
de Rest / Womenswear designer, Simone
Sassmannshausen / PR Manager.
8th row
Rosemarie Hup / Office Manager.
9th row
Sjoerd Borneman /Production, Vivian
Holla / Store staff, Steven Pooters / Event
Manager.
10th row
Miguel Mohamadjar / Store staff, Jason
Schragger / Marketing Manager.

Location: "For our friends" store.

BLUE HOLDINGS
March 30, Pacific Palisades,
California, USA

Left to right:
Jimmy Taverniti / Designer, Taverniti So
Jeans, Benjamin Taverniti / Designer,
Yanuk, Sophie Wizman / Brand President,
Antik Denim, Taverniti So Jeans and Yanuk,
Beth Guez / Owner, Blue Holdings, Paul
Guez / Owner/ CEO, Blue Holdings,
Philippe Naouri / Designer, Antik Denim,
Alexandre Caugant / Designer, Antik
Denim.

Location: Home of Paul Guez.

DIESEL
May 16, Milan, Italy

President Renzo Rosso with Diesel store
staff members.

Location: Via Manzoni.

EARNEST SEWN
March 8, New York City, USA

Top row, left to right:
Douglas Babbit / Executive Vice Presi-
dent, Commercial Director, Carlos Qui-
rarte / Director Of Business Development
& Strategic Marketing, Tatum / Carlos'
Shiba Inu dog, Ben Smith / Denim Design
Development Coordinator, Jared Seavers
/ Graphic Designer, Sara Brenner / Design
Development Director, Yan Liang / Head
Patternmaker.

Bottom row, left to right:
Lori Jacobs / Vice President Sales & Part-
ner, Scott Morrison / President, Designer
& Partner, Karobo / Scott's Rhodesian
Ridgeback Dog, Eleanor Ylvisaker / PR
Director & Partner.

Location: The Earnest Sewn shop,
Meatpacking District.

EVISU
March 13, New York City, USA

Left to right:
Nick Starsmore / Director USA and Global
Retail, Peter Caplowe ("stand-in") / Mana-
ging Director, Nicola Scagolari / Director
Licensing.

Location: Evisu showroom, SoHo.

FIRETRAP
April 24, London, UK

Front row, left to right:
April Taylor / Men's Accessories Designer,
Belinda Desoer / Fabric Technologist, Vivi-
enne Peak / Black Seal Graphics Designer,
Lee Sedman / Men's Collection Designer,
Sophie Clinch / Females' Product Director,
Asbed Momdjian / WDT CEO, Nick Hayes
/ Black Seal Designer, John Vivian / Men's
Product Director.

Back row, left to right:
Carlos Singh / Marketing Manager, Colin
Clarke / UK Sales Director, Mark Dale
/ Supply Chain Director, Sally Joyce /
Females' Designer, Pam McCrone /
Females' Merchandiser, Petra Heide /
Export Manager.

Location: The Prince of Wales pub.

FORNARI
May 15, Civitanova Marche, Italy

First row, left to right:
Monique Soeterboek / Commercial Dept.,
Giuseppe Stroppa / Retail Dept., Serena
Sessa / Retail Dept., Alessia Vita / Mar-
keting & Communication Dept., Caterina
Aimone / Fornari Marketing & Commu-
nication Director, Lino Fornari / Fornari
Director, Giusi Fornari / Combo Director,
Roberta Cingolani / Marketing & Com-
munication Dept., Elena Dini / Executive
Assistance, Nicoletta Russo / Marketing
& Communication Dept., Francesca Ma-
chella / Executive Assistance, Annamaria
Domenella / Marketing & Communication
Dept.

Second row, left to right:
Patrick Micalizzi / Manufacture Dept.,
Alessandro Bisconti / Commercial Dept.,
Cinzia di Bello / Retail Dept., Andrea
Sanchioni / Commericial Dept., Stefano
Torresi / Business Dept., Emanuela Pe-
trolati / Personell Dept., Mario Atteritano
/ Marketing & Communication Dept.,
Roberta Ermini / Marketing & Communi-
cation Dept., Letizia Mignini / Marketing
& Communication Dept., Jenny Macellari
/ Marketing & Communication Dept.,
Marco Taddia / Marketing & Communica-
tion Dept., Mario Smorlesi / Factotum.

Third row, left to right:
Fabrizio Cortigiani / Project Dept., Paolo
De Sanctis / Commercial Dept., Yongbae
Seok / Design Dept., Catia Moschettoni
/ Commercial Dept., Raffaele Primitivo /
Graphic Dept., Chiara Pacinotti / Com-
mercial Dept., Lugi Davi / Design Dept.,
Carmelo Canaletti / Administration Dept.,
Maura Santancini / Marketing & Commu-
nication Dept., Sara Gaetani / Marketing
& Communication Dept., Francesco Tulli /
Marketing & Communication Dept., Um-
berto Alessandrini / Commercial Dept.

Location: Fornari headquarters.

FREESOUL
April 17, Florence, Italy

Left to right:
Francesca Cozzi / Personal Assistant to the CEO, Sana Jelali / Area Manager North Europe, Vincenzo Morganti / Human Resources Manager, Paolo Dari / CEO, Luciano Galeotti / Logistic Manager, Michele Lopez / Brand Manager, Andrea Montanari / General Account Manager, Harald Jacob / Fashion Director, Riccardo Gori / Customer Service Manager, Manuel Menini / Area Manager South Europe.

Location: Freesoul headquarters.

GOLDSIGN
March 27, Los Angeles, USA

Founder Adriano Goldschmied with his wife Michela and their daughters Glenda (front right) and Marta.

Location: Goldsign laundry atelier.

GUESS
March 22, Los Angeles, USA

Left to right:
Maurice Marciano / Chairman of the Board, Paul Marciano / Vice Chairman of the Board and CEO.

Location: Guess headquarters.

JACK&JONES
April 30, Brande, Denmark

The entire Jack&Jones team.

Location: Bestseller headquarters.

KEANAN DUFFTY
April 2, New York City, USA

Left to right:
Nancy Garcia / Partner & CEO, Keanan Duffty / Designer, Patrick McDonald / Muse, Devo Ino / Design Assistant, Charlie Green / Make Up Artist, Simon Collins / Consultant.

Location: Telephone Bar & Grill, East Village.

LEE COOPER
April 24, Twickenham, Middlesex, UK

Left to right:
Marta Diggins / UK Commercial Assistant, Antoine Roy / Group Creative Manager, Audrey Beylemans / Group Marketing Services Manager, Karim Bouhajeb / Group Trade marketing manager, Aki Paphides / Head Designer, Mark Ainsworth / LC100 Group Designer, Earl Pickens / Lee Cooper 100 years Project Consultant, Narinder Kaur / Group HOUR manager.

Front left to right:
Lesa Bonner / Senior denim product and develoment manager, Andy Rigg / Group executive head of the Brand.
Picture on t-shirt: Tim Browne / Group head of design and development.

Location: Filthy's at The Red Lion pub.

LEVI'S
March 28, San Francisco, USA

First row, left to right:
Kayo Mitsuyama / Levi's Design, Caroline Calvin / Senior Vice President Global Creative Director Levi's Brand, Janine Chilton-Faust / Vice President Levi's Design, Loreen Zakem / President Levi's Brand Wholesale, Steve Evans / Vice President Levi's Brand Men's merchandising, Jennifer Roye / Levi's Design.

Second row:
Levi's Design team: Andrea Chynoweth, Heidi Baker, Cir Sayoc, Lorena Gutierrez, Danielle Puller, Karen Potesta.

Third row:
Levi's Design team: Brigid Malabuyo, Trev Yoder, Nada Grkinich, Jill Guenza.

Location: Levi Plaza headquarters.

MARITHÉ + FRANÇOIS GIRBAUD
April 20, Paris, France

Left to right:
Charles Bachellerie (guitarist of "the amazing the"), Morgane Bachellerie (sister of Charles; both are the grandchildren of Marithé), designer Marithé Bachellerie, Olivier Bachellerie (CEO and the son of Marithé) and designer François Girbaud.

Location: Gibus Club.

MAVI
May 2, Istanbul, Turkey

Left to right:
Ersin Akarlilar / CEO, Elif Akarlilar / Global Brand Manager.

Location: Galata Bridge.

MELTIN'POT
April 11, Matino, Lecce, Italy

The Romano brothers Salvatore, Cosimo, Carmelo and Fernando together with their cousin Ezio and Cosimo's son Augusto.

Left to right:
Salvatore Romano / Manager Product Development, Augusto Romano / General Manager, Cosimo Romano / President, Carmelo Romano / Manager Planning and Production, Fernando Romano / Manager Research and Development, Ezio Romano / Director Administration and Finance.

Location: Meltin'Pot headquarters.

MUSTANG
April 26, Künzelsau, Germany

Left to right:
Managing Director Heiner Sefranek, his wife and managing director of Bogner Jeans, Jacqueline Sefranek, and his father and company founder, Albert Sefranek.

Location: Mustang Denim Museum.

REPLAY
April 10, Asolo, Treviso, Italy

Owners Paola Buziol (Member of the Board of Directors of Fashion Box Group) with daughter Silvia and son Gianpaolo.

Location: Garden of Buziol Villa near Asolo, Treviso.

RIFLE
May 17, Barberino del Mugello, Florence, Italy

Owner Sandro Fratini with his entire team.

Location: Rifle headquarters.

SIXTY
April 16, Rome, Italy

Wicky Hassan (Co-founder and Creative Director, seated center) and Renato Rossi (Co-founder and CEO, without a mask on the right in a gray polo) with Sixty staff.

Location: Sixty headquarters.

TOMMY HILFIGER
May 8, New York City, USA

Founder, Head Designer and Chairman Tommy Hilfiger (r.) and CEO Fred Gehring.

Location: Tommy Hilfiger headquarters.

TRUE RELIGION
March 29, Los Angeles, USA

Left to right:
Charles Lesser / Director of Special Projects, Chana Taft / Director of Retail Operations, Pete Collins / CFO, Michael Buckley / President, Jeffrey Lubell / Founder, Chairman, CEO & Creative Director, Daryl Rosenberg / COO, Rodney Hutton / Senior Vice President of Merchandising, Gonzalo Posada / Production Manager.

Location: True Religion headquarters.

VANS
March 24, Huntington Beach, Orange County, California, USA

Left to right:
Ashley Moltz / Girls' Accessories Manager, Shannon Kennedy / Girls' Apparel Graphic Designer, Luciano Mor / Guys' Apparel Category Director, Mike de Wit / Guys' Apparel Graphic Designer Steve Van Doren / VP Promotions/Ambassador of Fun (son of company founder), Tyler Ash / Surf Footwear Manager.

Location: Vans Pier Classic, Huntington Beach Pier.

INDEX

IMPRINT

Editor & Publisher | Klaus N. Hang

Executive Editor | Sabine Kühnl

Managing Editor | Wolfgang Lutterbach

Art Direction | Alexander Lorenz; Gianluca Fracassi (shoot "A Family Affair")

Production Editor | Christopher Blomquist

Design/Art Work | Art+Work=Werbeagentur, Frankfurt a.M.

Production | Sacha Majidian, Swami Sprecapane (SI Milan Office); Hans-Jürgen Wulf (DFV Frankfurt a.M.)

Contributing Editors | Fay Cantor-Stephens, Melanie Gropler, Regina Henkel, Maria Cristina Pavarini, Michaela Schmidinger, Barbara Stockinger, Tim Yap

Contributing Writers | Guilherme Aquino, Kim Benjo, Martine Bury, Michael Cohen, Lisa Dartmann, Nicole Fall, Akiko Hamaoka, Emma Holmqvist, Jelena Juric, Anna Kirby, Karin Leiberg, Barbara Markert, Lucia T. McCarthy, Kevin McGue, Max Padilla, Lincoln Phillip, Miriam Rayman, André Rodrigues, Arianna Shetabandeh, Benjo Wylson

Photographers | Marco La Conte (www.marcolaconte.com; shoot "A Family Affair"); Zacharie Bauer, Gabriele Galimberti, Alexander Gnädinger, Anthony Hill, Sebastian Rosenberg, Erik Swain, Martin Veit, Jelle Wanegaar

Translations | Jennifer Hackney, Berlin

Marketing & Distribution | Christine Zeine (Director Marketing & Distribution, zeine@sportswearnet.com), Caron Banez (Marketing Manager USA, banez@sportswearnet.com)

Editorial Offices Europe | Via Forcella 3, palazzo c, I-20144 Milano, Tel. +39 02 58 16 91, Fax +39 02 89 40 16 74 | Mainzer Landstraße 251, D-60326 Frankfurt/Main, Tel. +49 69 75 95 2672, Fax +49 69 75 95 2670, editor@sportswearnet.com| Editorial Office USA | 580 Broadway, Suite 701, New York, NY 10012, Tel. +1 212 925 1240, Fax +1 212 925 4795, editor.usa@sportswearnet.com

Advertising | Advertising Sales | Pierre D'Aveta (Advertising Director and Sales Northern Europe, Tel. +49 69 75 95 26 64, daveta@sportswearnet.com),

Valarie Anderson (Associate Publisher/USA, Tel. +1 213 627 0256, anderson @sportswearnet.com), Jeffrey Molinaro (Senior Advertising Manager/USA, +1 212 925 1240, molinaro@sportswearnet.com), Maria Bomboi (Senior Advertising Manager/Southern Europe, bomboi@sportswearnet.com, Tel. +39 02 58169 305), Anna Cumerlato (Junior Advertising Manager/Southern Europe, cumerlato@sportswearnet.com, Tel. +39 02 58169 318), Anna-Lena Mikoteit (Assistant Advertising Director and Sales Northern Europe, Tel. +49 69 75 95 26 63, mikoteit@sportswearnet.com) | Advertising Services | Maike Sprungk, Tel. +49 69 75 95 26 62, sprungk@sportswearnet.com

Subscription of Sportswear International Magazine
(6 times a year + Who's Who + Trade show guide „it's showtime")
www.sportswearnet.com/subscribe

Litho | Selescan 3, Milan; Uwe Wöltchen, Art+Work

Printer | Franz Kuthal GmbH & Co., Mainaschaff

CD | Softloop, Frankfurt a.M. (Design and Programming)

Publishing House | DFV Publishing Group, Mainzer Landstraße 251, D-60326 Frankfurt/Main |

Managing Directors | Dr. Rolf Grisebach, Peter Kley, Michael Schellenberger

Supervisory Board | Klaus Kottmeier, Andreas Lorch, Catrin Lorch, Peter Ruß

Cover | Fifth Avenue Shoe Repair

Additional copies of this book can be directly ordered at:
www.sportswearnet.com/whoswho2008

If you require further information please contact us at:
whoswho@sportswearnet.com

ISBN 978-3-86641-118-0
© 2007 by Sportswear International, Milan, Italy

THIS C...
...SIVE GLOE...
ON THIS CD (...
INFORMATION TH...
IN THE ANNUAL PRINTED VERSION OF WHO'S
WHO, INCLUDING PROFILES OF AND CONTACT
INFORMATION FOR MORE THAN 550 OF THE MOST
NEED-TO-KNOW FASHION BRANDS/COMPANIES PLUS
MORE THAN 500 RETAILERS, TRADE SHOWS, PR FIRMS
AND FASHION-RELATED MEDIA OUTLETS. AFTER INSERTING
THE CD INTO YOUR COMPUTER, USE THE DROP-DOWN BARS
TO THE RIGHT TO SORT THE DOSSIERS AND FIND EXACTLY
WHAT YOU ARE LOOKING FOR. YOU CAN SEARCH BY SEC-
TOR, COUNTRY OR BOTH. WE HOPE YOU ENJOY THIS NEW
TOOL AND TRUST YOU'LL USE IT OFTEN THROUGHOUT THE
YEAR. THE INFORMATION ON THIS CD IS ALSO AVAILAB-
LE ONLINE ON OUR CONSTANTLY UPDATED WHO'S
WHO DATABASE. SPORTSWEAR SUBSCRIBERS CAN
ACCESS THE DATABASE ANYTIME, ANYWHERE
BY LOGGING ONTO OUR HOMEPAGE,
WWW.SPORTSWEARNET.COM.